NOW IS THE TIME

THE TEACHERS OF THE HIGHER PLANES

Fourth Book of Wisdom

Ruth Lee, *Scribe*

This book is an updated and revised version of the 2006 edition originally published by AuthorHouse.

LeeWay Publishing
Naples, Florida USA
www.LeeWayPublishing.com

ISBN: 978-0-9970529-3-0
Library of Congress Control Number: 2016956729
Printed in the United States of America
First Printing 2016

Cover design by Sarah Barrie of Cyanotype.ca

More Books by **Ruth Lee**

Other Books of Wisdom From The Teachers of the Higher Planes

We Are Here

The Work Begins

The Art of Life ~ *Living Together in Harmony*

The World of Tomorrow

Bliss is It!

The Word of The Maya

The Making of a Scribe ~*How to Achieve a Life You Can Write About*

Can You Pray? *We Are All Here to Seek the Way*

Writing in Spirit Workbook

Writing in Spirit Notebook

Novels by Ruth Lee

Angel of The Maya

Within the Veil ~ *An Adventure in Time*

Writing in Spirit ~ *Jeanne's Story*

Dedicated to teachers of wisdom
Wherever you may be!

Introduction

There is no time but NOW, yet many think otherwise. Why? They are lost in time! Time exists only in our minds—and within this single existence in the universe. **Now is The Time** explains why time exists and makes total sense of it!

The Teachers of the Higher Planes, channeled by Ruth Lee, answer the great, age-old questions about time and life as it exists only in this world, providing in-depth explanations about things you may not realize exist now. A marvel-filled experience for anyone seeking to transcend this life—and ascend at the end of it.

This is your opportunity to change your life within a few hours! One quick read and you will want to go back and read it again more slowly—then again and again because you missed so much in the past.

To learn more about ***The Books of Wisdom,*** *The Teachers of the Higher Planes,* and *The Scribe, Ruth Lee, visit*

www.LeeWayPublishing.com

NOW IS THE TIME

The Teachers Of The Higher Planes

Fourth Book of Wisdom

Ruth Lee, *Scribe*

Chapter One

Who you are is not a problem for most. Where you are going is the stumbling block. Why you want to succeed is obvious, as well as knowing how to get there, but deciding what you want to accomplish seems to be a lifelong pursuit—rather than the beginning of lifelong adventures. Why?

When you are the only one on Earth, you fear no one, but if one other appears, you begin to sense you have competition. This sense of competition carries you to the point where you decide within whether or not you should fight or take flight. Birds take flight, but men tend to fight, and women usually settle into a battle that may take years to determine who is first in whatever.

If a woman is not in the prime of life, she may let others take precedence over her and lead, but all others struggle to dominate. The picture of women being docile and complacent is erroneous. Women are and always have been fighters—and warriors are not known to take captives.

To become all she can be, a woman needs to learn to adjust to others who want similar goals—letting them seek their goals in peace and harmony. What no woman needs is aggravating circumstances or people prodding, or pushing her and making demands. She can do that well enough herself.

To enter your life into the machinery of humankind and see it fit and work well is not of interest to most women. To experience admonishment for poor work or bad behavior is not wanted, either, but work today neither suits nor benefits most women. To grow, a woman has to fit in and feel beloved, or she enters into constant battles for supremacy over other women.

Why would women fight women? To be at the top of the list! '*You never know who you are if you are below others*' is the rationale used today—which is not why most women struggle. Most women want to be loved—and being loved is not easy today. Too many expectations are imposed upon even the simplest of women's lives.

What you decide to do with your life is all that matters to you. So why get involved in the lives of others? To closely examine and see how you measure up is the prime reason, yet the outcome usually upsets and disturbs those who do it. They see only the discrepancies and values of others, not the similarities and idiosyncrasies that make them different. The values of another are of no concern, but their achievements often upset you. Why?

Jealousy is the end result of measuring yourself against others and determining you are not as good. Why measure others if you end up hating them—or yourself? You either have poor measuring tools or your values are not valid. It is no big deal to recalibrate a poor measuring tool, but if your values are not sterling, you may as well give up. Reevaluate your life to determine if you would be upset with your best friends upon comparing your life to theirs. If you get upset, you have a problem.

Perhaps joking about differences is the best way to diffuse energy that would otherwise concentrate on one person, but not the way to enter work you must do to become a better person. Ridicule often stops people from being themselves. It can be used as a cruel means to keep others in line. Beware of the comic who leaves a sting!

You will find a little bit of the worst left over at the end of a line and within humankind. If the last in line or on the list is not bad, you have a long line of grand people. If last in line is a pest, mean, nasty or vicious, the entire clan becomes suspect. This extends to families, companies, clubs, churches, or any organization.

If you wish to enter a life beyond this one, you need to associate with people who believe in God. It is no big deal, but too many bring up other issues that can surround and overwhelm that simple fact. If you live alone, believing in God is not difficult, but add another and you get into debates.

The key debate is primarily about how to worship. You need to worship according to your life and style, but if permitted to do so, others will disagree and try to impose their standards on you. Do not let anyone tell you how you must worship. It is your right to live and worship as you wish; however, you have no right to tell others what they must do. This can lead to war!

When you war with others, you lose, even if you win. The only loss you can afford is money. You cannot afford the loss of face, pride, or time. Time on Earth is short and does not afford you a wide margin of safety. You have only so much time to do your work before you are called back to review your life—so get busy NOW!

The trials of life are both obvious and consistent if you do not face up to them early and pass through them when young. You may be faced with dilemmas of power struggle between parents or siblings at the tender age of two or three—but if you can satisfactorily resolve them then, you have it made. No more will you have to struggle with it, but few learn that quickly. Most go through life trying to avoid such nerve-wracking situations over and over again—defeating themselves.

To face a situation headfirst is not the same as facing forward. You need to know which is best for you. If you are to remain unscathed, you cannot face forward—thus missing side action. If you wish to rush headfirst into action, think it out before you advance. This is needed NOW!

Thinking out a problem first requires knowing who you are and what you can do. It also requires knowledge of all participants. If you know not yourself and never cared to learn about others, you now have a problem, and that problem is yours all your life.

Thinking of only one solution is a problem for many. You have to be flexible or break. The fragile thing about human beings is the mind. If it breaks, you cannot easily assemble a new one. If you want to foolishly break into the minds of others in order to defend yourself, you could end up being broken and discarded. No one bothers with those who cannot think for themselves. They have no sense of who they are, thus cannot be trusted.

You must be trustworthy...
You cannot learn it from a book!

To be trustworthy comes from the real *you*—not the schooled, disciplined you who reads books and attempts to train and develop self to become the best of all people. You cannot train people to be honest, dependable, or trustworthy. They just are! If you learned a person is neither dependable nor honest, how can such a one be trustworthy?

Many teachers believe: '*Adjust your thinking and you will believe as you are taught*'. It is not true doctrine. People do not adjust to the basic values of life. Values are present at birth and developed and polished—not given at a later date.

'*Born to be bad*' is an accepted belief among primitive tribes, while modern man scoffs at the idea. How else can you explain differences among families? You cannot! Let others be—live your life and expect nothing from others. You can be *you*, so let others do the same. Once it is the way of the world to let all others be, the world becomes one.

Evil and good are two parts of the same thing, but not the same. You may feel evil, yet do good in order to attain an evil goal. Would your efforts be considered good or evil then? This is a way to evaluate it:

> *Visualize your life as an open basket and see if anything looks shabby. Before going further, identify what needs to be repaired or discarded. Examine the bottom of the basket to see if there are any loose ends needing to be knitted together to prevent them from unraveling. If any, knit them together. This is the way to sort through all the affairs of your life.*
>
> *Once your life is in order, examine how you train your children. Do you still spend time on them? Do you care if they love others and are loved? Do you want them to succeed—or are you slightly jealous of their success? Do this culling and sorting with each child you brought into this world. Once this is done, you are done. There are no others in this world you have any responsibility or right to observe and attempt to change their behavior.*

When you work in the world, you often reflect the home-training you received. You also take the world back to your home, so be careful of the work you choose or it may poison your nest. In the work-world are many of diverse backgrounds who think differently and act unacceptably to you, but you must learn to tolerate them if you are to access the next plane when you cross over at the end of this life. No one has to adopt the behaviors of others or even accept their values, but you must permit them to continue as they do or be guilty of bigotry.

Bigotry is not the word used to describe a personality unwilling to accept others as is. It is the word used to describe your actions when you refuse to accept differences in others. Never apply this label to others, since it reflects *your* standards. If you are a bigot, you will see it in others, but not yourself. If you are a thief, you see thieves wherever you go. If you frequently use such a term to describe others, do not assume you are not a bigot or thief.

The only time to wage war is when you no longer have any other option—and your life is being threatened. You may wish to war long before then, but you will never win a war you have no need to win. The need to win is not the same as needing to war. You need to win if you war all the time, but the war thrust upon peaceable people must be won. There is a difference, and if you do not see it, you are warlike.

Warlike people are predominantly in cities and states where there are no rules. If rules are used to instill peace, they are good predictors of the temperament of the people and their ability to accept differences among themselves in order to have greater good for all. If rules are used to confine only certain people, they are of no use. People will rise up and overthrow dictators in time. Dictators are of no use in times of war if they know not what to do—and they are never necessary in times of peace.

What you do with your time is what counts
—not who is in charge

If you want to be in charge, you must give up much of your time for the good of all—which is not why most want to be leaders. To be a leader does not automatically instill respect or awe in the minds of those who follow. You have to lead an exemplary life, cater to the whims of many, and follow your heart—all at the same time. Do you still think you can do it and maintain a schedule? If so, take your place at the head of the column. You are needed now!

The only good leader is one who knows what to do, how to do it, and why it must be done. All who merely talk are idiots. You must never turn your life over to an idiot to run it for you. You will notice idiots are often given responsibility to run high offices in a land by people of great sense. Why? Laziness and greed are not the only reasons for poor judgment, but are foremost.

You are lazy if you refuse to acknowledge you do not do all you can and have time left for others, but choose instead to waste it on fun and games. Greed is not the only reason you want others to do the work and run the show, but a way to avoid being caught with both hands in the cash register. You may not think paying people to run a country is evil, but how else can you evaluate the system that protects no one.

The only one to run you and your family should be you, but a common response of those wishing to control others is that they may not be able to distinguish right from wrong or know enough to feed themselves. Why would God let anyone have a family if they could not in truth feed and clothe them? It is not God who chooses such a family, but the individual.

If you chose to be born into poverty, why would you expect it to be otherwise? You may expect big things from life, but life is exactly what you are and will be. You are your life! You create it each and every day. If your life is great now, you need not change anything. If you need clothes, start sewing and darning what you have—and work harder to earn money to buy new things. It will be yours before the next season arrives. The same is true for all your needs.

If your life is not as you planned,
You did not plan!

You cannot plan and work for something that never works out. You must concentrate on life and visualize your future—then sit back and let it materialize. If you do that and nothing happens, you are not of God! God would never let it happen. You blame God for all that goes wrong in life—which is totally off-base and wrong. You need to instead bless the day you found God, and promise to be of God, before you say God has not blessed you and taken care of your needs.

Once on the right track and your life is flowing freely, you will know it and have no further regrets. Until you straighten out all that remains amiss within your present life, you will not have peace. Peace comes only to the warrior! The warrior does not look for war, rather is the one who wars when necessary to maintain peace.

Whatever you need, you will have it—and whatever you want, you must earn. Decide if it is worth it. The last of the worst of the most despicable human beings on Earth will be the one who blasphemes God—but the one who wasted this life will be out in front.

Chapter Two

The only world you know is the one in which you are concentrated in now. If you can dissolve into another world and another, you know there are many more, but most of you cannot do this. To be able to dissolve into another world is not to be achieved by the undecided or un-complex. It is accomplished only if indefinitely pursued for an express purpose—otherwise it is too dangerous to attempt.

Danger is not of this world. Danger exists in the mind—not of spirit, but ego. You often frighten yourself by simply watching television programs or movies. What would happen if many people tried to enter your life? You would become confused and direct much energy toward something of no value to this life.

You are in this life now to be ready for the next assignment—which hopefully is on a higher plane. If your work here is incomplete or poorly done, you will be sent back to work it out again. We see no way to avoid such a turn of events if you do not concentrate on your life in the present.

Having explained it, you need to absorb it!

Do you realize the difference between one half of life versus the other half? Do you know when you open the door into difficulty or ease? Can you tell in advance if you are going down the wrong path? No! You have to explore your mind until it becomes clear. If you physically rush to do something, you lose.

Work first in meditation to explore every aspect you need to be aware of—before you go forward with it. When you can decide which of two works you wish to concentrate on, you are half-way to your goal. If you have more than two alternatives to consider, you have much work to do to narrow it down to two.

The rush to complete work today is not of the world, but of God. When you feel you are behind schedule, you are! To be on top of your life, you need to be free of such constraint.

The only time to become aware of work you are doing badly is when you are doing it—not after it is done. Once a job is completed—totally done, it requires tremendous effort to reenter and erase what is of no use or is now invalid. Before you begin—and certainly before you end any work, ask God if the work is complete or needs more effort on your part.

Your friends of this world are not here to lighten your work, nor are you here to help them do their work; rather you are all here testing different scenarios together to see which path is quicker, easier, or more pleasant. You never know if you are on the right path until you are somewhere along the way and see no obstacles; however, you can see the path before entering it if you back off and view it from a high place. You can do this through meditation. Work on meditation now!

If your life is not your life—and for most reading this that is true—sit still. Do not move, talk, drive, or think. Sit still and let life catch up and play with you now. Once you can see how little you know, but have to know, you will work.

In the work world are many who plan to take over the world, which is too ridiculous to contemplate now. No one has ever taken over the world or even half of it! It is a fool's dream. Work on you—and if ready for the next plane at the end of this life, you have won the world.

Now that women are no longer *'chained to their kitchens,'* as some still say, are they rulers of the world? We question the sense of such a goal. Why be a queen of the world if your family does not know who you are and never sees you? The work of the world is merely a pastime designed to keep you in enough money to live. It is not your real work!

Which world do you live in now? One is solid and material, but the other is real and true to *you*. It is where you dwell all the time, only lifting yourself out of it to do chores in the material world. You live there all the time and are known only to you there; however, in the material world of make-believe, you exist in many different aspects. Why? Because you need something to occupy your time as you progress through this episode on Earth.

Earth is not the only planet inhabited by people of high intelligence—and not the only place you live now. You dwell here in *normal* working hours and elsewhere when asleep. You do not sit still and let the dream come to you, you go to the dream.

The time you spend dreaming is not lost, but not remembered much. You may feel it is wasted time and try to deny you dream, in an effort to prove you do not waste time—know that you are busy as you dream. Your dreams carry you into the upper spheres and help you adjust to Earth. It is not easy to live on Earth! It is no longer a healthy environment, and is much more negative, so you grow and develop elsewhere.

The work of your life is not over when you accomplish all you came to Earth to do. Once this work is done, you are expected to prepare for the next life, and the next. This is the normal order of progression, but today many sit back and relax at retirement and totally ignore the rest of the world they are still attached to both physically and spiritually. This is why there are so many more people today who struggle constantly. The only ones who know how to successfully traverse life are unwilling to help those still moving along the path. Shame to all who neglect their fellow man!

What to do is not hard to explain, but why you do it is difficult. Sit now until you understand these words:

> ***I am not of Earth! I live here, but I will not be here long. I have a responsibility to my host. I have been negligent and need to now help my host repair damage caused by my present existence and any power wasted on me.***

Do you feel a sense of despair now? Do you think this cannot refer to you? Do you sense God watching what you do? All of these are incorrect reactions. As a personality living on a planet that encourages you to help yourself, you should know you are not to take advantage of your host's graciousness. If you have abused Earth, restore what you abused until life is in balance. No need for great remorse or repeated prayers, just work to undo your mismanagement of precious resources.

The only time you need worry about the weather is if unprepared for whatever. To know a storm is coming and remain unconcerned is terrible. In order to protect life and property, you need to take precautions. You are in danger if you do not know a tornado is headed your way.

Before building in a place where violence or bad weather is common, take time to contemplate such danger. If it is your desire to help those who foolishly wish to live there for unexplored reasons, you may proceed—otherwise it is best to leave such conditions and places now. You are not to help others remain in a place where it is dangerous to live. If you would not live there, do not encourage others to do so.

If you believe in urban renewal, live in the city!

Why you are here has little to do with why you live as you do. The choice of home, situation, and friends is left entirely up to you. If you choose friends who are not like you, you do no harm or good. However, you would be better off choosing a close friend who had experiences that complement your own—but not necessary. You may prefer to live with those very much like you. Why is that? You prefer them to others because they will not subtly encourage you to change your ways. To change your ways is not difficult, but not desired by most.

An Earth change is one which causes the concrete reality of this life to loosen and shift, and consequently remove doubts about who you are. You cannot remove the contents of one home and place them in another without discarding much that is unusable in the new place. You, too, are like that when you grow. Be ready at all times to move, but you may never have to move to grasp the truth about *you*.

Once in a while the work of this world changes for everyone. It is noticeable only after a hundred years or more, but it becomes obvious. You are now in such a time!

Your work is changing from large, high-overhead businesses to small, personal enterprises, as in former times, so you can realize your full potential. The *'old world'* was great for learning humility and taking pride in your work, but the new work is better. Think on these things:

1. You do not own your work.
2. You cannot sell your work.
3. You have to earn the respect of those who serve and protect your income.
4. You cannot be lazy or you will starve.
5. You cannot become servile or everyone will tire of you.
6. It is not easy to please everyone, so learn that you must please *you* every day—in every way.

Much of the private world of strangers is closed to you. If it was open, why would you want to know about it? You do not have much time to get involved in the life of one other—let alone people unknown to you.

Today's television programs inspire no one. They pillage and loot the lives of celebrities and stars of many realms in order to feed the insatiable appetite of the lax and lazy masses. You must not be a party to such worrisome worlds.

If you cannot inspire another, sit quietly and smile. The effort to smile is greater when times are uninspiring, but such effort does produce miracles in others. If you must, from time-to-time place your life in the hands of your Spiritual Guides, but always resolve to lead your own life.

If you carp and nag, you are not helping anyone. You actually harm your being. Please refrain from this type of negative activity, because it is caused by your attempts to control others. You are here to live and breathe—then move on—not to raise many children and control their lives until no longer possible. That is not parenting!

Whatever you do now is present in your entire being—wherever it is. If you do not hear us now, you are not reading. If you hear us here and now, sit quietly and stare at this page.

Why sit and stare at what does not speak? A television set does not speak, it transmits the words of others—but does not speak for itself. Speakers are not of this world and usually not present in today's media, but they will be in years to come. Right now you do not wish to adopt a new way of learning that incorporates and uses media and books to teach spirituality. Books will remain the choice of scholars and friends of *The Word*, but most others will adopt easier means of communication.

Work is no longer a place to share ideas, rather a place where people constantly compete, thus it is easier to talk via computer—never seeing anyone, even those few you admire. Perhaps you know them now—perhaps you do not, but you still talk. It is time to reinvent your life and live!

Whatever you do, do your own work!

If you lie, cheat, or steal from another, you never advance. Wherever you took something from another, you are left with huge gaps within you, so let others advance rapidly when you cannot. Let them move on to other fields.

You are *you* and doing your work here! This is where you are and where you will work now while keeping in mind:

1. Never force something.
2. If you cannot do it now, set it aside and it will come to you later.
3. If you cannot make it happen or fit, it is telling you to try another approach.
4. Be open to suggestions, but not swayed by everyone who passes judgment without consideration of your problems.
5. You know who you are—or you should, and others do not.
6. Ask nothing of others and they will not waste your time.
7. Be kind to those who trust you.
8. Do not offer suggestions that are not well-considered.
9. Do not enter into others' competitive frays with the intention of defeating them, it will backfire.

In the evening you are not as tired as you think you are. You experience flashbacks of the day's events—which is how your life ends. You may look like you are tired or worn-out, but merely reviewing the life you led and examining it for flaws. If your life has been a rewarding experience, your old age is not a time of jubilation—rather a time of peace. If your life left many things undone, you may be petulant or irritable—but not unhappy. You never regret until you are on the other side. That is when you know it all!

While you sit and stare at open space before you, do you see anything? You can if you learn to open up to your inner vision. Why not try now? If you could see the old, new, and all the other work going on around you, would you become confused? If so, let it go until later.

When your life is over the hill—around the bend, and the next episode is being formed, would you like to know why you came to Earth? We would like everyone to remember why before they depart, but it is not always possible to break bad habits. If you are not open to new ideas, why not accept old ones? Because you do not want to change!

If you see yourself as a baby or prone to reject the idea you chose to come to Earth—even chose your parents, you will not like the idea that babies you meet everywhere are more in touch with God than you are, but it is true. Think carefully before you reach out to touch a baby. It is of God. You are of God, also, but you are not as fresh from God as any baby, so do no harm to such a little one or rue the day you were born.

Now that the time to change is here, you definitely do not want to change! You fear it will interfere with what you have and that you will lose if you do not continue as is. Why? Why be afraid of losing what does not satisfy you? Look into the future. Look there for anything you do not already have and you will see it is still there. You change in order to add to your life—not subtract from it.

Get out a notebook and list your life's ambitions and goals as of today. Put down all your dreams, and listen to your heart. Why not be all you dream? Why not have all you want? You alone hold you back. We are here to help you change what does not let you move forward, but it is up to you to change NOW!

Put your mind into high gear and let it all roll now. You deserve to be here on Earth, and you deserve to leave it as a big success. *Be you NOW*!

Chapter Three

The woman or man who is not ready for today is lost! If today is not finished, you cannot be ready for tomorrow. You have to work every day as it comes to you in order to be ready to ascend at the end. If you sit on your work or ignore it, you will be left at the starting gate waiting for the next race.

To race about in many different circles can increase your endurance, but if you are not centered, it can lead to much confusion. You cannot seek answers or gather information from only one source and expect to know all there is to know about a subject. To absorb information and then seek an expert is usually better than hunting within circles of less than high quality.

We will help you center your mind now!

Before you can learn anything, you need to center your mind. Put your hand on your forehead. Do you hear yourself thinking? No, you may hear your ego talking, but you cannot hear yourself thinking. Your thoughts go deep within and require much persistence to be sure you are correctly tuned in to your wisdom. We are not Guides, but we can tune into your thoughts. If we can do it, so can other beings.

What you need is to learn to hear your thoughts, *then* learn to tune into others. Once you can do that, you need not listen as closely to what others are saying to understand every word spoken. To tune into another person is not done to be intrusive, but to learn from them. You will never intrude if you first ask for permission to do so. To ask, simply bow your head in the direction of the other person and silently ask for permission. If that one bows to you, you have the privilege of tuning into them then. This is practiced in various cultures, but not in the West. We are aware that many who bow are unaware they are giving permission to others to enter their minds—but they are.

Put your hand on top of your head now. Do you feel anything? Is there any heat there? Is light visible there? No, but you know energy is entering and leaving this area, you just cannot see or feel it. Now you will notice it seems less dense. Fear nothing and it becomes lighter and brighter. If afraid, this energy source becomes closed, tight, and produces headaches.

If you are cramped, the old way of warming your hands in order to cure a headache is still of use, but the best way is to totally relax. Let your hands fall into your lap and sit still. Do you have any difficulty moving either hand? Do you sense a problem? If not, sit and let all your feelings and fears run out through your hands, then shake them as though shedding water. You should be totally free of negativity then. When you become covered in negativity, wipe off the exterior of your body with water and soap or shower. You need not enter the water to be cleansed.

Whatever you do, do it with fervor!

If you are to be of use to the work you must do on Earth, you need to know your life is good and worthwhile. Work on the day of the week you can do the most work and do all you can then. On the day of the week you are least likely to produce much, list all you can do even if tired. Do those things that day.

You have high peaks of energy and low spots, but you always have energy. To increase your energy requires many people around you who are also high in energy. You can be drained by people who dwell in darkness and only enjoy the light of others. You must avoid them. Your energy is not limitless. You have to be all you can be and do all your work, thus giving others your energy and receiving none in return is not for us. We will help you avoid such people.

To put your life on hold while you help others is never wise. You can help others, but your life has to simultaneously go forward. We note that when some people help others their energy soars. Fine—if it works that way for you, otherwise do not do it. Let each person realize the need to be in charge of their own life—and help them take charge, but do not do their work.

All your friends and neighbors may now notice a change in you. Why? Are you suddenly nicer—friendlier? If so, you need to expend more energy helping others now. Continue being less than available if they sense you are no longer a '*patsy*'. It is time to balance your personality as it works and interplays with those closest in distance to you. You can see energy enlarged and decreased by the space between objects and people. You can control your ebbing and flowing energy. Do it now and live many more years in good health.

If your home is a place where you can find no rest, it is absolutely necessary for you to change it drastically or move now. You cannot afford to live any longer where you are not *at home*. Put out the dog, put out the cat, put out the milk bottles, and get going. Change your life NOW!

What you need to be safe and sane is not what you need to get along in the world, but it must be present. You must know *you* and be you! Once you know *you* and are you all the time, all this life is the best so far.

Think of all you do and all you want, and you are there! It takes only a short time to manifest, because it is there. Work fills the time.

Now that you know about work and that time is merely a way of expanding your life to the point where you are aware of it, you will want to learn to use time to fill in gaps in your other lives—but you cannot do that now. Now you must live while on Earth and do all you came here to do.

When your life today is complete and you have time on your hands, do you sit and watch others work? If so, you lose. Help them do their work and it will manifest as your work, too. You will learn to do things of great use in your future. We often present you with opportunities to learn first-hand what you will need tomorrow. Have you noticed?

If this life is not the only life you live—and it is not, how do you think you can be out-of-body here and in a body there? You cannot. You are here—you are not there. You live in this body and can leave it alone for short periods, but you cannot move it into another space.

Put your life into a little bag and see if there is room for another person. Do you see enough room? No? Then do not harbor doubts about someone else entering your body. If you saw plenty of room for more people to enter the little bag, your mind is not fully developed and your body is not as developed as it should be. Get to work on your studies and exercise now!

When a person has a large ego, it can become so blocked by egoistic pursuits that no one else can enter that life. This is now happening all over the world! People do not want to marry or have children, because their egos are swelled out of proportion to their importance to the planetary workings of the universe.

If you send out a message to the furthest planet, when do you think you will hear back from it? Not in your lifetime. How far can this egoistic society be heard? As close as we can tell, a bit over a half hour. It is that shallow!

Your life is never as shallow or deep as the world, but the world is a reflection of you—not *you*, but you. If your real self is deficient and unable to accept God as the ruler of the universe, you have a long way to go before you realize you do not matter much. Each person on Earth is a microcosm of the universe—but is not the universe. You need to understand that truth before you can continue.

Prepare for the next day today and tomorrow is a left-over today. Let tomorrow go now. Do not worry or fret over it. You need every minute of today to do all you must get done now. You have time tomorrow.

Put your arms out to your sides at shoulder level. Do you feel any pain or tension? No? Good, you are in shape. If you feel any pain, tension, or pulling, you need to exercise more. All the exercise you need is to be free of tension and pain—and build endurance.

Why spend hours building muscles which do nothing? Vanity! Other people's admiration, and work on the body, does nothing to advance your spirit. Work of the world is seldom worthwhile. Enjoy your body and use it well, but never be a slave to it.

If your back is injured, do you continue to walk? No? That is good. Pain increases in the back if you continue to walk. Rest restores an aching back! Rubbing it and exercise are of no use then. Do not argue about the body, let it restore itself. If traumatic injury occurs, you must seek drastic remedies, but otherwise rest is enough.

When you rest, do you sense the world is busy? Do you feel absorbed in a cocoon or other place of rest? Do you wish you could be up and about as usual then? You will feel all of this once you are well.

You need to overcome the tendency to rush forward when you are not well or your body is not ready. Rushing hurts! People tend to hurry if they fear. If you are afraid you are late for an appointment, you hurry, you fret, and you get angry. You are not happy. Why not be early and save yourself much stress?

If your time always runs short, you are not accurately judging you and your lifestyle. Since you are the only one living your life, why not know how long it takes to get dressed, eat, shower, etc.? You must understand you before addressing other issues of life.

Many traps are set in the work of the world by those wishing to make it to the top quicker than others. Why? Greed has led them to believe they alone need money. You believe everyone needs money to live on or buy necessities; but do you believe: If one person has it all, the rest go without? No, never.

God is responsible for your needs. You must take care of your wants, but your needs are provided. Never run over others to get what you want or they will run over you to get what they need.

In the work world of today are many who are not working. You may be aware of it or not, but it exists. Once all workers cease to work, who will pay for all their needs? God! You have never paid for needs. Your food is provided. Perhaps your clothing is not as you desire, but it is provided, too. Ask anyone for a dollar and they will give it to you, but ask for $500 and no one in their right mind will give it to you merely for asking.

Ask God and your needs are given!

If you can sit and read, we assume you are not tired, but many read when tired in order to fall asleep. Why? Why not fall asleep and later read to fortify your mind against the future? You know your future! You know your past. It is *now* you do not know.

In each person's past is a long period of yearning to be free, but once free, where are the opportunities you once dreamed about? Dreams must be concrete in form. Dreams must be organized in time and space. Dreams must be practiced ahead of time to occur in sequence. You can have all your dreams or none of them. It is up to you.

If your day's work stretches into the night, you may say you worked overtime, but if you worked only a few hours, you did not. Sense within you a schedule of the hours you prefer to work, then make sure to keep it. We will help any who need time to schedule their lives.

If your day is too short to complete your work, you cannot do each day's work correctly. Be sure you trim off unnecessary work—or lengthen your day. Your work must be done! No work can be left over to do the next day or your life becomes spiritless and dull.

Wherever you flow or go, you will sense much excitement around certain people. Do you flock to them, too? No? Why? Do you fear them or are you jealous? If you cannot approach one of God's own, you must be either afraid or jealous. God gives a glow and certainty to certain members of the flock so those straying can see at a distance the direction they should be taking. Be sure you never stray too far from the source.

If your work day is over and you have time left, use it wisely to promote your wellbeing. Your future is then the best it can be. We will let you mull over this material and ask only this now:

When will you be free of worry?

Chapter Four

The only one you cannot trust is yourself? You can trust others only as far as you trust yourself—no farther. The only one to trust is you! Put this into the phraseology of your mind:

You are not the only one on Earth!

The above phrase sounds as though you made it up, but you did not. You learned it from the spheres. You learned to use words as easily as you learned to speak, yet most of you never heard words until you came to Earth.

The time spent on Earth learning new words is atrocious. You should have learned to speak and walk within days of entering the gravitational pull of Earth, but did not. Why? You chose to dawdle here on Earth and learn at a specific rate.

The time you have on Earth was assigned to you by the *Lords of the World*. You have no time to dawdle here NOW! You must work hard on your life and leave enough time to develop a few lessons ahead of your next life. If you waste time and do not develop into all you came here to be, you will have no time on Earth left to do it.

Ease and leisure are bywords of American society, and many others think it a wise way to live. You have only to observe how much damage has been done to this society by following that path. It is the wrong way!

To develop, you need to leave your past behind every day. You cannot drag it forward and taint every new day. You have to learn what is important and necessary and leave all else behind. If you seriously believe you cannot go forward if you leave all behind, at some time in your life you must learn to face life without anything.

In the event you learned that lesson, but then let it slip, you will be haunted by the need to move. You will learn no more of the past and your life will bend. If your life is bent now, you cannot see beyond the bend and are unable to fully appreciate all *you* are. Each night as you fall asleep, work on dropping your past. All you need to know is stored in your memory for any important occasion when you might need it—usually you never need it again.

If your life is not flowing smoothly, you may wish to dump on others who are smooth in their approach to life. If you do this, you will soon be dumped. Do not enter others' lives in order to ruin their way of life or to cut into their energies. You have enough of both.

In the future of this life are many avenues yet to be crossed and many streets still unknown to you. If you do not have a map, you will certainly get lost. Be sure you know where you are going before you leave. We are not able to draw up a map for you or help you do it. You have to lead your own life!

The time and place to begin drawing up a map is wherever and whenever you are ready to change direction. If you do not know who you are or where you want to go, how can anyone help you?

The only way to do it right is to sit down and analyze your dreams. You can ask others for theirs, but all you will get is their life in a diluted version, which will prove to be <u>*most*</u> unsatisfactory to you.

Whatever the time, you have only enough to get to the other side. You cannot call people and tell them how to live their lives, then expect to have time for yours. The telephone has ruined more lives than it ever saved in an emergency. Why hold up busy people? Why speak then of things you cannot say face-to-face? Why not ask for a visit? It is easier to rest and never face the fact you are lying and cannot stop while talking on an instrument where you never face the other party.

Wake up! Get your life moving now!

Do not wait for time, be ahead of it. Get your life in line to increase the welfare of others, not take it away from them. When not responsible for what you say, the ability to deny is far greater, and most people do not feel responsible for what they say on a phone. You need only hear the hum above Earth to know it is polluting the atmosphere—and some pollution is of the earthy variety. Work on cleaning up your act and never having to return to Earth.

If your conversation is not directed at anyone or anything, why talk? We want you to concentrate on you now—not on others. If you talk only of what you know or need to say to get life going, you will not tie up lines for more than a few minutes. If you hang onto the phone set longer than that, you know you are wasting time—and time is what we are talking about as being in short supply. Are we not?

If you talk about others during your conversations, do you know them? Are you personally in contact with them? Do you believe they know you? If none of your answers are positive, why talk about them?

We want you to spend time on *you*—not on people unconnected to you in any way. If you waste time in such pursuits, you will surely end up behind time. The only one who cares about the time of day is someone behind schedule or is conscientious. Which describes you?

To work all day at a job that has you watching a clock is not work—it is drudgery. You need to work until the job is done without thinking constantly about time. The time it takes to do a job is enough. To spend hours longer trying to fool another is foolish. You need to spend time on your life, not on such work.

Working on yourself should take up most of each day, but seldom appears that way. We are telling you that if you do not work on self, you are not living. You have to feed, clothe, and rest your body. You have to educate and defend your life. You need to know all you can about why you are on Earth and what you came here to do, which takes up all remaining time. You do not have time to sit and chat about nothing of consequence. If you do, you will miss something important.

Meditating helps you physically, mentally, emotionally, financially, and spiritually. What else can do all that for you at the same time? Nothing!

Meditate to save time!

When you meditate alone, it takes less space in your day, but isolates you from others. If you meditate in a place of worship or in a room filled with others also seeking peace, you can accomplish several human needs at the same time. The need to: assemble, socialize, and connect with other spiritual beings.

We would like you to join or form a circle of people like you and find a time that suits all, so you can meditate as a group. Group meditation helps beginners and advanced elders alike. It puts you in the center of a group and forces you to acknowledge you are not alone on Earth.

Only once while on Earth do you realize life here is unlike life anywhere else outside Earth. You have chosen to be here—why? To describe it more clearly, let us speak as a one who is not very bright might say it:

> *You are here to learn why you came here. If you never find out, how can you leave? You do not! You came here to do something—and you have to do it, then you can leave. If it takes you fourteen lifetimes on Earth to do it, you take in fourteen times this work. If you learn quickly, you may be here only a few times, but it always takes time.*

Time is of no use to us. It is a measurement you choose while here to divide a life episode so you can decide where you are at any given time. Some decide to end their life episode earlier than planned, and some ask to remain longer. It is out of the ordinary, but you may even be able to ask for a change of lives.

The only one who cares where you go is your *Chief Guide of Spirit*. This Spiritual Guide is not attached to anyone but you and has a definite interest in seeing you get to the other side of this life and not have to return. Each Guide has been chosen to work with an individual for several reasons, most involving spiritual development; however, there are times when an individual must return for purely materialistic reasons.

If the Spiritual Guide you worked with was to leave you half-way through this life, who would know how much you accomplished? No one else cares about this life as much as you and your Guide, but others are also assigned to assist in this earthly passage who would help you; however, you would be handicapped if this happened. As a Spiritual Guide, why risk helping anyone who would do that to you?

You do not walk out on your Spiritual Guides! You can walk out of this life, but not leave You. The only one who can live in this body is another aspect of You. All others who live with you on Earth or elsewhere are not of You—but related to *you* in some way.

If you do not know who *you* are or why you came to Earth, you should seek to find it out immediately or risk having wasted this life. If you waste a life on Earth, it may not be here the next time, and thus cause you to regress. If your life is going to flare up and down like a flame in the wind, you must catch it and cause it to settle into a constant heat or lose it.

You must never ask others for help if you do not need it—including your Spiritual Guides. You never have enough time, but believe others do? That is selfishness. Do all you can when you can and all will be done. If anything is missing or undone, call for help. To receive help indicates you have not been working at life, but to let help go because you are not seeking it is no indication you are working on your life. Be sure you know who you are, then go after the rest.

We want you to be ready for the end of a life episode so you can enter the next life without a long wait in-between. This will speed up your time spent on Earth. Some get so immersed in this world that they want to stay after the body dies away. If you cannot understand you are to be reborn, you cannot understand you are not dead. At least learn this lesson now, so your soul will not wander around after you go elsewhere.

Some people call it *reincarnation,* but it is not. Reincarnation would indicate you died—and you never die. Although born again in another body, you did not die. You take on different forms, but remain the same soul.

You do not need to experience all your lives as the same person, only the poor of spirit have to return again and again to relive the same life situation in order to learn who they are. All others advance into different areas of Earth at different levels of development and seek experiences as different people of different race, sex, and cultural status. This enables all to know the full extent of life on Earth. Whichever level you are now, you will know you are no different from others only if you once experienced their background.

You never tire of being you, but may tire of being a woman, man, or a certain race. You cannot change these things. It is that way for a particular reason. You chose to be exactly who you are, and to undo it is to harm yourself. Work on self-acceptance first, then life is less a problem.

If you hate who you now are on Earth, you face the worst possible problem. You have to learn to love you— then learn why you did not—and then learn to get on with your life. Why not shove it all in a box and say: "*I love me. I want to be all I came here to be. I'm ready to be me now*"? Once you say it—and mean it, everything old is cast aside and never again worthy of your time.

We are not old women or men. We are not even young, but we know! We know you, and you do not know us. We definitely have the advantage now, but we never take it. Do you take advantage of others?

If you cannot lose or you expect to win all the time, you constantly take advantage of others. You must let others win and lose, too. Many adults today are hung up on being ideal workers or ideal parents, but few try to be both. To adults who do not care if children learn about life, letting children lose is not a natural behavior; but to help children live the best possible lives then and as adults, it must be learned.

Parents who live their lives as best they can, helping their children grow in God, are the best of all people; but any parent who refuses to dwell in peace and harmony—with God in the forefront, is of no use to us or the world in such desperate times as these. More damage has been done by useless parents than anyone on Earth can possibly imagine.

The world is being destroyed by parentless children—who may actually have a parent! If parents refuse their responsibilities, Society must provide for their children. A society that does not care for its children cares not for anyone!

Your life is never over because you made a big mistake, but refusing to acknowledge the mistake or letting others know of it, you could end your days here as a misfit and have to repeat it all over again. Learn from mistakes and make proper restitution, then begin again as if no error occurred. This is the way to live.

The worst of times in any life is usually remembered afterwards as being the best, so enjoy such difficulties if at all possible. If you can be you and live through bad times, the good will long outlast the evil of all other events combined.

If work is done in the vein of a workman doing his duty, it is never evil; but if evil is done in order to get workmen to work, nothing good will come of the work. Never coerce others to work! They either work or do not. It is their decision. You must do what you must do, but you cannot force another to work for you.

Slavery of old still exists, but more mental or emotional now and not as physical as it was. If you or anyone you know enslaves another, you must free that one. If you do nothing to end the enslavement of others, you are not held directly responsible, but you will be watched to see what part you played, or not, in freeing them.

Today drugs are the primary way to enslave another and are freely distributed in America and most other countries. Why? It reduces the effectiveness of large segments of the population no longer needed to work for others. Work is not created for the masses anymore; manual work is being reduced to the point where most have none. You will be blessed if you create jobs for others—and quite the reverse if you substantially reduce their opportunities.

Once lives are destroyed, where does their time go? It is nonexistent, thus adds up to nothing. Your life is not enhanced. In fact, you may be unable to leave Earth, because you aided others in enslaving the masses. Work is not an opiate, but it occupies time required to be spent on Earth.

If your time does not pass rapidly, you are not working. If it flies by as fast as the second hand on a watch, you are busy. Work—for time is fleeting and you cannot leave Earth before all your work is done by you!

Chapter Five

The only time you can waste is time you do not use to further your inner life now. Time provided is to be used productively to promote the work of your soul. If you waste time leaving your path—so much the better to teach you a lesson, but no help is given by us then. If you waste time while trying to find your path, usually you are not helped much, either.

The help people often seek and expect from above is not really help—rather intervention in some worldly matter where they want to gain an advantage over others. This is not a godly principle, thus not obtained through us. If you need advantage over the Godless who practice unhealthy or immoral ways of obtaining gain—regardless of the plane we are in, we all help.

The time to learn about the planes above *you* is when you are ready to use that knowledge, not when you begin your journey here. Before you are ready to end this episode and go forward into the next test, you must first traverse all of Earth.

We would never tempt you to end this life in order to get to the next one. It would be the condoning of suicide, which is against all earthly religious and moral principles. You are here on Earth to learn to abide by the rules and regulations of your society and world. You chose it, so you work with it. You succeed or fail. It is a test you set up for yourself, but you were given Spiritual Guides to help you get through it. You do not go through this life alone, but you alone get credit for all you did.

No one else can be of use to you at the end. You are the only one there then, and you are judged individually—not as a member of a clan or any other group. You will answer for your life, and get nothing for helping others, unless they offer you their blessing when they pass over. This particular blessing is of special importance in instances where a soul may be lost or have to return to Earth and this blessing is such that they are spared.

If one *dies,* as you say, on Earth and gets no credit for anything, that soul must begin again and return for another chance. If that soul does not do it all again, the chance of being permitted to continue in that plane is gone. This is where the blessing of a dying individual who remembers such a person and gives him or her a spiritual gift can spare that soul from having to return to a lower plane.

If you were the only soul in your world now, you would have no world. You have to have experience—and experience is of the world. It is not of God. God is! God cannot be experienced. You are of this life, but God is and never *not*—you will know what is meant.

If a life in the present is lost due to an accident, many people assume the individual was taken before their time, but that is not true. All go at the time they stated before they entered this plane, but some are granted an extension if their work is close to being done or they worked hard to better the entire world. You cannot say people did or did not do what they came here to do—only they know that within their deepest mind.

If your life is your life, you cannot ask others to decide for you what to do with your life. Some ask continually for help and guidance—why? You know *you,* or you should, yet you ask daily for help and guidance. We are of the notion it is merely a habit and means very little to you. If you do or say something that means nothing—it is just filler. Put your mind to removing it and end such wastes of time now.

Talking continuously to people can be of help or it can be a hindrance to all concerned. Determine first if you are helping or not, then cut out the chatter. Chatter is our word for *'not of any use'.* You can be of use to us if you have nothing else you need to do, but first be sure you have your life in order before asking to work on godly projects.

We cannot say your work is of God, but others will. We want you to know there are several days of prayer in each life that determine the man or woman, and it is the days of prayer in which you live and dwell in God that determine your life. You cannot be baptized without prayer, or be married in your religions without prayer, but some do not want prayer, thus ending their religious lives. That is not the end of religion, however, nor is it the end of prayer in an individual's life. If it were, there would be no world today.

People pray to God, but seldom think of themselves as being of God and capable of answering their own prayers. If you see yourself as God, you are in serious trouble; but if you know you are *of* God, you are on the path of truth. The path is not difficult, but some refuse to accept it is there, preferring to stumble through life, falling into dark crevices that break their spirit.

God will lift out of darkness any who are there; however, if you prefer to stay in the dark, you may. It is your life to live as you wish, and at the end you are placed in your own way of work. Some return to Earth in order to develop, while others return to work-off a bad life experience in which they misdirected themselves or others—and some are returned to help others who may be lost, but able to be saved.

Decide which category you fall into and perhaps it will help you understand your role this life. We care not. When you are in a role, you act upon it in every area of life; but if you remain flexible and willing to switch parts in order to learn about others who are also learning, you can accept life much more readily.

To fight life is to lose!

You have to return again and again if you lose. You are not here to best others or amass great wealth. You are here to learn how to live as you are and enjoy it.

Self-mastery is not self being taught to accept others' will. It is teaching self how to live as good as possible within a given situation. If there are enough people around you to watch and observe your behavior, you learn as much in a cage as in a large organization. Cages are made by man, but organizations merely exist. You cannot randomly amass several hundred people and expect them to coexist. The ability to do this ceases around the number ten or twelve, beyond that you are in large groups that must be organized.

Organization is to the world what planes are to the universe. You are organized, developed, and presented to others of Earth as a group known by your joint efforts. If you work for God, all revere you and trust you, but if you work only for yourself no one cares.

Put your life in the balance and see if you can locate where your ego is. *Hint:* It is the airy part of you. It has no substance, yet is full of wind. It is the talkative you, the braggart within you, the difficult personality, the spoiled brat, the negative one who condemns you, and for the most part—is not of God. You will struggle most of your life on Earth trying to control and rid yourself of negativity, but the ego is your only battle this life. Get your ego under control and life is a breeze—not a desert wind.

Whatever you do, and like to do, is done fast and efficiently. When you dawdle and wander about aimlessly, you either are not amused or do not like what you are doing. Change the work or change you, but do not let your work drag, because it will drain you of energy needed to do all you must do today. If you cannot get everything done, you have only this life now and maybe another chance, but there are other planes you must traverse, too. You cannot afford to spend all your time on Earth when you have so much more to do elsewhere.

When people ask: "*Where do we go from here?*" Do they really want to know? No! It is a rhetorical question. Do not waste time asking questions that require no answer or the answer is not going to be heeded if given, you are wasting your breath.

To believe you have only so many breaths is to believe you can earn a long life by mastering breath control. It is helpful to master breath control to maintain good health, but it will not extend the time *you asked* to have on Earth to accomplish this mission. On other planes you are fully aware of how little time there is here, and are fully capable of judging how long it should take to accomplish your life's goal, but once here you stagger and reel from one area of life to another seeking others to tell you why you came here. That is the biggest waste of your time here!

The only time another can tell you what to do is if you enable another to enter *you*. Since no one on Earth is capable of doing that, how do you believe it can happen? We know you believe there are *beings* and *spirits* who can enter the bodies of others at will, but it is of no use. It is a superstition that denies you have free will, therefore it is false. Rid yourself of stupidity and free enough good sense to go after your life's work now.

If you read about life, you may learn aspects otherwise denied you in the physical state, but you could also dream them. If you spend time daydreaming, you will be chastised by the public, but not by us. We are unable to enter your dreams, but your Guides do it to help you realize life is interconnected. You must learn this lesson!

If you lived in isolation and had no one to help or receive help from, would you care? We think you would become sick of mind and body if you did not care. We see you fail and fall down only to reawaken and begin a life filled with service to others. Why? Because you know it is *The Way*. *The Way* is easier than any other path, but yours is different from all others. Believe in that and you will be able to tolerate all while here.

In the work of the world are many traps set to snare the unsuspecting and un-expectant, be sure you know your way and set your course around these traps. What traps? Ego and greed are huge traps to avoid, but jealousy and hate can stop you cold, too.

In the world are many of all faiths and creeds, but few are devoid of the sins of the flesh. You must be alert and on guard for those who would use the roles of Earth to disguise their real intention of being less than of God. If you suspect, look and see if your suspicions are correct and make appropriate decisions.

If you are incorrect, be sure you are not wasting time suspecting honest people of dire deeds while letting others prepare or do evil before you.

If you know the ways of Earth, you can avoid a lot of trouble—or so they say. But if you learn the ways of Earth by experiencing them all direct, you probably will never be ready at the time you cross over. It takes time to experience things—and lessons are short. If you will ever be ready to cross over and move directly to the next level, you have to absorb, listen closely, partake of others' experiences, and learn to be full of goodness and faith.

We suspect most who try everything are not interested in advancing beyond this plane, thus will not be here much longer. You may not be privy to such information and become immersed in their lives and try to imitate them to your own misfortune.

When ready to advance to the next plane, all is explored. Based upon what you accomplished in this plane, you are not expected to go over each and every detail, your personal mountains and valleys will suffice. You need moments of greatness and self-condemnation to be able to judge life and live it now, but to dwell on the past or resent the future is surely a waste of energy. Time for that comes at the end.

Time is not of you or Earth

Time exists only on Earth, because it is part of the structure that contains and confines you to a single space and place in the continuum of universal laws. You do not have to know why there is time or space, but how to use each. If you lose your way, retrace your path and go to the next branch. If you go far along the wrong path, it can take your entire life to find your way back to the main road. Merely sample things along the way—do not get lost!

Demands are not our way, but we do make demands as teachers. We cannot stop you from doing anything. It is your life! You will be on the path of life or off it, it is your choice. No one else can tell you to sit or stand. You will decide if it suits you to do either.

Only diseases of the body can prevent you from physically doing things. The mind controls disease, so be of clean heart and mind if you wish to control the body in all things, otherwise the body will resort to dire measures to expunge all you wrongly did to it.

When your life is over and done, you will wish you had time to do many more things—right? No, you will only wish you had found God sooner and had more time to enjoy life. The only people who regret doing something are those who did not do well in life. Some may wish they had experienced life more, but hardly indicative of the many who are grateful for the ending of this life and their ability to advance beyond it.

What you learn is not as important as how you learn it. You need to learn things in a calm, collected way so you can recall it at times when you need it. If you haphazardly go into a class and learn everything in no certain order, you cannot recall it at test time—let alone use it now. We suggest you sit down and organize your time to best help you recall whatever you may need in the future—then forget all of it.

What you do in one relationship is of no importance to other relationships. You are not the same person to any other, so you do not need to remember anything about other people when with another now. To dredge up past relationships constantly in order to decide if you are changed or if this person is much like another is a terrible waste. You cannot try and convict another person for someone else's crimes, and you cannot work on this person to make them do what someone else neglected to do for you in the past.

Help others, then go forward!

If after helping others you stand around waiting to be praised, your ego made a big hit on your soul. Do not wait for praise for helping another. If you have harmed any being, wait until someone comes to settle the score—then pay your fair share. What if the score is too high or you are asked to pay more than your fair share? You still pay! You have created the initial *sin,* so pay! Due to such penalties, be careful in all of life's dealings.

Whatever the weather or climate, you will not always have favorable times to work. That is a fact, so learn it as early as possible. You cannot use weather as an excuse—ever! Put your work in order, and if weather permits, go out and enjoy the sun or fresh air—otherwise sit and do your work.

Loafing and idling are two terms you use to describe people unwilling to help others. You never use such terms to describe workers taking a break, even though these terms are synonymous with refusing to work. Are you loafing or idling away your life today?

The only time you have to do your work is NOW! You may or may not be here tomorrow. This is said so many times in a life that no one believes it, but it is the one absolute truth.

Chapter Six

The only time you have is when you are here. If you wait until tomorrow, you will never have time. *Tomorrow* is a term for what will never be—and used to procrastinate. If you plan on tomorrow, you will not finish today.

This is your time. Do all you must do, all you want to do—and be all you can be! It is not the time to think, but the time to be. '*To be*' implies you must do, but '*to do*' does not imply you must think. Combine both and you will be centered on *The Path*.

The Path is not a broad avenue or a winding trail. It is the impulse direction leading directly to the God source. If you do not enter the proper impulse—instead go off on a tangent, you may live your entire life in orbit and never enter God of All. This is a waste of time and will result in reentering this scheme and planning another life all over again—with the possibility of missing the mark again. Get on *The Path* now!

After an evil person enters your home, do you bar the door? No, you usher that person out and slam the door shut. In your mind you will often be tempted by evil. Do you throw out such impulses and slam that door, too? Maybe, maybe not, but it is your mind and your decision to keep it. It is not the '*devil*' or any other man-made idea that made you do it—*it is your idea.*

Putting distance between you and evil ideas is better than most other ways to handle it, but the best way is to never get involved. If you avoid all evil, you can at least avoid some of what is in the air, as well as most that exists around you. If you avoid someone not of God, you will not necessarily change them, but they cannot change you. That is the best way to remain pure of heart.

Purity of heart and spirit is the prerequisite of a good life. You need to be free of covert ideas and beliefs that undermine your work. If you believe and speak as one, you will find it much easier to remain stress-free and cool; but if you live one way and talk another, you will soon be upset and have to draw up a lie or live another life. Either way is difficult and need not happen—just live what you believe!

To do a lot of thinking on a subject does not make it worthwhile. You could spend years thinking only about a subject that has always been known to mankind. Would that advance you or mankind? If it can, fine—but if it is merely an exercise in stubborn egoism, you are on the wrong track.

When you find yourself traveling at a great rate, do you worry it might be in the wrong direction? If you do, it probably is. The mind is equipped with radar that intensifies the Guides' work of *The Spirit*. If it is said through channels that you are not on the right track, the mind will worry over it indefinitely until you slow down. Before you continue your journey, place that idea in the arena of all possibilities and see if another is not more feasible. You could save your life.

'*Time is of the essence*' is a motto that speaks of old and young ideas and work, but speaks not of *you*. You must be able to do whatever it is *you* want to do if you are to enjoy life. If you are to enter the kingdom of God, you cannot madly rush about doing others' bidding—not finishing your work.

The kingdom is within *you*—not in the world, but this is your life to do as you see fit. If you choose to dwell in squalor, it is your life and you may do so. No one else need worry about you, since you do not. If others choose to select you as a model of ugliness, you can adjust to it. If you choose ugliness as your model, you will die of internal bleeding of the clotted spirit. You need to run free internally. You need to be mentally free.

To be as free as you can be,
You need good health!

Take care of your body! Do not worry that it is in charge, because it is not. Your body is a free agent. It can and does take air and water and mixes them with elements to create life, but it is not using us or *you*. It does it all. You merely supply the necessary elements on a timely basis and mix it all with proper exercise. If you do this, there is no problem. If you exaggerate all these steps, you end up in trouble, or at the very least, in a state of *dis-ease*. If you let up on any one of them, and do not act in a responsible manner, you will not have good health. No big deal to figure this out, but some never do.

Your body may look good to you, but another sees flaws in it. So what? You do not have to look at you. If another dislikes you for how you look, you have lost no friend, but discovered an enemy. Think and be thankful for that knowledge.

In the future of all who dwell on Earth is a time when the elements will be depleted and no air will remain here. What do you think will occur then? You are now here, but do you care about those who will be here in the future? You should, because you do not know if you will be returned to Earth and be here when the end of air becomes a reality to human beings.

What you need to know is why you waste. If you can determine why, you then can do something about it. If you do something to curb waste, you will help keep depletion levels from becoming extinction levels and ending your world now. It is a joint decision based on the attitudes of many who care—or do not care. If you care, you can find many to support you. If you do not care, do nothing and join the majority.

The majority of souls here now are not inwardly concerned about mortality, yet fear death. It is a strange, contrary way to view life, but it exists in most societies today. You can enjoy life every day and be ready for its end, or you can fear death every day and never be ready. It is your decision.

Whatever you do, you must not do it for others. Do it because you want to do it, you like to do it, or you wish to change—then it is yours, and you will enjoy love and life. To love life is to live. You must never hate anyone or it will turn you into an object of hatred. If you dwell on hate, it changes and devours you—not the object of your hatred.

Turn your life inside out and you will see snarls and knots cover the underside, but the top looks beautiful. No matter what you think now, it is the act that counts. The only time you need to work on you is when you are alive and well. Once you pass over, you need not worry or work on you, because it is all over. Until then, you have time.

Work is not so difficult that it cannot be done, but you are difficult and may not want to work. There is quite a difference between work and drudgery. Drudgery is never liked, but is often required to finish the details of a job. It builds character, but never joy.

Work is a joyous time. You feel great and it helps you. If it is something you love to do, work is not work. Be sure you work—then any drudgery is not as long or as difficult.

While living your life on Earth, you may not be aware of time. You may not know who is here or where they are, but some in spirit are with you here on Earth. You may never actually meet them, but know their work. You recognize it as your own, because you are in the same channel. You think and act the same. You do all your chores the same way, too. Do not despair if your other has more money or fame, because you are there, too.

If your friends in spirit are unable to connect with you, how do you get in touch? You are in touch with all souls. You are in a gigantic network of electrical impulses that surround the universe. You need only channel into one to know it exists.

Once you can channel into one source, you may believe you are great, but you are not. You are merely a channel of a source known to many. If you could channel, who would you wish to connect with—Jesus, Buddha, Mohammed, Mary, a saint? Think hard and you can. If you do, you will be able to connect!

In your life are many who are not connected to anyone or anything—or so they say, but you know differently. They cannot be here and remove connections from the universe from whence they came. You are also connected to this world. This world is a creation of man and not the work of God. It is the work of many people who think and create an atmosphere in which they thrive, survive, or are challenged. Which do you choose? You may never know as long as you live here.

Thinking of things is not the same as actually doing it, but to do anything requires thinking. If you do all your thinking before you set out to do whatever work needs to be done, you may take a long time planning, but the end result will be accomplished in exactly the same time as others who plod along and do not think ahead.

The danger of thinking out all actions beforehand is that you may not actually do it. If you do not act, nothing is accomplished. You have to do the work!

Whatever day of the week suits you best is the day to devote to *you*—God is then a part of *you* here. If you never devote any time to God, you will end up depleted—not God. God is energy and light—life requires both to bloom. You will die an early death of spirit if you never use your sense to accomplish all you must do—and then rest. To rest is to refresh your spirit, and your spirit is of God, so set aside a day to refresh.

When you rest, do you expect others to comply and rest, too? Do you think others should shut down when you do? That is not the way of God. You must do what you must do, but all others are here to do what they must do, too. If you force your doctrine upon others you are actually imitating a god—which is blasphemous.

You are not a god and never will be!

If you turn on an instrument of control, and it works, do you turn it off? If you let a media control your thoughts, are you better for it? We think you are smart enough to know that you alone know what is best for you, but there are those who think otherwise. Think for yourself NOW!

In religious orders of the world are many who believe themselves to be above the population and take no active part in Society's everyday life. You may also harbor such elitist beliefs. You will discover you are seen to be the same as everyone else on Earth. You are of Earth. If Earth is not as you would want it to be seen by all others in the universe, do all you can to change it now.

To enter into seclusion and dream of God is not an elitist practice, but one which empowers the individual. You may dream of God and never know it, but if you take a drug or concentrate on this quest, anything you see may look like God to you—but is it?

What you see is not necessarily what is. You have eyes to help you evaluate facts and figures and defend you against agents of ill will, but you may not have eyes to see into the heart of another. It is not the eyes that see, but the intellect behind the eyes. You must develop that intellect if you are to know of the life of one you look at. If your intellect is strong, well-exercised and experienced, you may have the wisdom to see—but may not.

If your life is an enigma, you are wise to seek a solution. But if the life of another is an enigma, you can safely walk away. You do not need to understand why others are as they are. You must know why you are as you are—which takes a lifetime.

We of the higher realms are not upset by anyone on Earth who is not of God, because they have so little power. God is of all and cannot be imitated. For men and women to spout wisdom to others and ask that they be honored by all as prophets or seers is to blasphemy God. This will result in a downgrade of that person's life. You must not help such a person destroy self.

Time is of the essence if you are dying and have not yet healed, but it matters not at all if you are not dying now. When will you die? No one knows! You must be ready is all we know!

This is the time to remember you must be ready. You have to be! If you are caught with half of your life still unknown, you will be unable to go forward. If you need time to do one or two small things, you can be advanced in time. If you ask for help, needing time to do all of the things still undone, you may be given years more, but not necessarily.

Time is of no use to others—only humans

In other planes you will learn other methods of dividing space, while on Earth time is your dividing line, so master it. If you cannot handle time, how do you expect to enter the world and succeed? You have to do it NOW!

Some of Earth's people are from old lineages and refuse to learn new ways. It is of no use to you to describe all the old ways if they no longer fit the new world. You cannot use all the old ways, but if some help you—go for it! There are many ideas in the ether left from times gone by which you can use. All you need do is sit and meditate, then ask for ideas you can use now and see what comes to you. It may be ancient wisdom—then again it may be new.

Use what helps you!

Many healers are in the world, yet many in the field of modern medicine are unfit to be healers. How do you reconcile this difference? Use both! Some people are great at only one thing. Why not use them to help if that one thing is something you cannot do? You will learn that all have a special *gift* left over from another time in their development that enables them to live as a modern man or woman. Seek out what you know and use it to help yourself NOW!

If your life is bent on destruction, you may not know who you are. If your life is dedicated to helping others learn who they are, you may never find your path. So if you want to be sure you are on T*he Right Path,* learn where it is and how to return to it at any time if you should slip off it. To admit failure is not bad. To continue to fail because you will not admit it, is dumb, dumb, dumb—instead be as smart as you can be.

Within your path are many ideals and ways to be you, choose only one or many—but be you! If you cannot discern what is best for you, seek people who are quite good at helping others because they learned how to do it. Do not waste time seeking help from those who are as lost as you are.

Put your faith in God and you will never be disappointed. Put your faith in *you* and you will seldom be disappointed. Put your faith in others and you will surely be disappointed—often. Work is not any different.

Now that this session is about to close, do you feel any different from when you began working on it? Do you recognize the difference between time and effort? They are not the same, but if either is wasted, the other is also wasted.

You must know *you* if you are to be all you came to Earth to be—and it takes only as long as it takes you to learn. Learn about *you* early, so you can enjoy a long life and not worry about death overtaking you before you are ready. Fear of death falls away once you know you are ready to go and can ascend to the next plane. Be sure *you* are ready NOW!

Chapter Seven

The end of time will come when all your life here is done. You will not know—but it will end then. The next plane has no need for time. You will be unaware of it, and your life on Earth will be a dream. The only one to remember it all will be You.

If this life is a dream,
What are dreams?

Dreams are time in a capsule. You dream of life in other times, places, and here on Earth, but it is all about *you*. You do not have to be someone else to enjoy your dreams, because *only* you can truly enjoy them. If this life is a dream, why not enjoy it? You can!

You need to write down all the events within a dream while you are in it. Since this is difficult, write out the details when each dream is over. You do need to be disciplined to do this, but it can be done without ruining your sleep.

Here is how you can begin to work on your dreams:

First, *place a tape recorder beside your bed near your dominant hand. Have a light available if you need light to write, but make sure it is dim. Once light hits the eyes, Rapid Eye Movement (REM as your scientists tagged it) ceases. If you instead talk through a dream, they will not.*

> ***Second,*** *after you wake up, enter your notes in a book. Ask aloud or write: "What does this dream mean?" Why ask? You need to know the answer. You cannot figure out all your dreams immediately. You need time to digest them—then have a new session. In other words, dream and ask...dream and ask...dream and ask. That is how to remember them, as well as what they mean.*

> ***Third,*** *ask what you should do with information contained in your dream. If you know what a dream means, you may figure it out; but then again, you may not. If you ask, you can get the true meaning of a dream and use it immediately.*

Many years of study have produced little information on dreams, because men are now unwilling to believe they dream. If you can produce important information from only one dream, why would the entire dream sequence not be of even greater use to you? Logically, you cannot deny dreams are of value once you know what they mean. So stop denying and get to work!

Some of the work you do at night is not in your dreams. You also work on your mind and body—never employing your dreams. We will demonstrate that now.

> *Put one hand over your open eyes. Can you see anything? Then close your eyes. See anything now? There is a difference when light seeps in around your fingers. You need only a little light to see, but a lot to explore all the nuances of being.*

> *Now put your hand in your stomach. You cannot do it, can you? Why? There is no opening directly into the stomach. You would have to cut into the abdominal wall and enter by way of an incision. This could be dangerous to all your internal*

organs. Why? Light enters then. You may not realize light often causes cancer to spread during or after such surgery. If you do not open a cancerous patient, the cancer spreads or grows much more slowly.

Why are we so interested in your stomach? Your stomach is a pocket of darkness. It is not open to air or light. It cannot empty directly into the air or light. Its contents are routed out of it and empty into another area before being evacuated. The stomach is so important that you must make sure it is cleansed daily. If your stomach is not clean, bacteria can accumulate and back up or overflow into other areas not equipped to handle it.

Why would you take time to cleanse your face, but ignore your stomach full of acid? Because you do not see it. If you must see everything before taking action, you will lose much this life. You must take some things on faith.

The end of this life is difficult to view, because you do not want to know about it. If you refuse to know something, do you stop the process? Hopefully, you now see how ridiculous this entire idea of never discussing death really is. Place it among your nervous worries and let us explore death with you more.

Do not work out a plan, or plot how to end your life, merely say aloud what is bothering you and ask for what you need to know. Work is always in process. The mind is never still—nor are *you*. Work of the mind is seldom of value to *you*, because it is totally involved in this Earthly stage of development and of little use to your entire spiritual being.

You need your mind to get out of bed and off to work or school, but what else? Nothing in life is absorbed by the mind. You use it to accumulate data needed to make a living, but it does not settle disputes. You are a spiritual being and need to set limits on how much time the mind is to take up during your entire life here on Earth.

Work of the Spirit is not as difficult as other work on Earth, because you are accustomed to doing it. You live in spirit and work within your mind, but your body lives only here and now. How else can you accomplish so much? We know all of you like to argue about integrating body, mind, and spirit without knowing anything about any of them. How do you know they can be integrated? You do not.

If you could integrate your mind and spirit, what would you achieve—a spiritual mentality or a mindful spirit? Neither is likely. You need time to believe in you and time to be you, but you do not need time to think. As your mind goes from one subject to another, you think constantly. Thinking never ceases until you learn to control your mind and make it subside enough so Spirit can be heard within.

If you meditate properly, you can hear your mind opposing Spirit. It is a constant battle for supremacy, as far as the mind is concerned. Do you hear opposition? If so, you are not alone. The ego is not strong—nor is it weak, it just is. Your spirit is not strong or weak, either, but if you put the two in opposition to one another, one will overcome the other's weakness and dominate it.

If the mind dominates spirit, you have headaches and pains in your head. You likely will be constantly worried and upset over details, and will not like people to get too near you. Your days will be constant battles to be on top. You know you are not doing your best, but never able to put together the reason. This is the pain of not being in touch with God.

If Spirit dominates the mind, you have no headaches and your mind is free of worry, *but* you may lose touch with everyday difficulties. Although you have no worries or cares, your mind has to be prompted to continue with everyday needs of holding down a job and living with others. If you ignore that phase of life, you obviously fail at living well now.

Balancing Spirit and Mind is the goal
—not trying to integrate them!

Why not live in your mind? You have a mind and need it, but not for living. It is a tool used to keep all your facts and figures in order so you can make a living or whatever you need to do daily. It helps determine whether or not you are alive or dead, but it cannot end your life.

If you cannot live in your mind, can you live in your spirit? No, you live in a minimal part of your body, but do not actually need all of your body to live. You could live with only a fraction of it functioning and not die. You are not completely contained within the body, but live within it.

What if the body dies and you do not? That is exactly what happens—you do not die! You simply move into another area.

You cannot stay forever in this body, but you do not have to leave Earth. You could continue living here, but why? To live on Earth after the body dies is not the best of lives. It is not a comfortable life, but can happen if you fail to realize you are not dead. Some souls are so unprepared for death that they believe they are merely sleeping or living in a dream when they are actually dead to this world. If you are to be able to easily cross over to the next plane, you must prepare your mind for the end of this life.

If your life on Earth is not what you want, you have all the resources to change it. Your mind can be filled with useful information and used to develop avenues of wealth or whatever resources you need to move out of your present situation or to know how to spiritually ascend. To ascend spiritually is easier than developing the mind once you are beyond your learning years.

It is not impossible to develop the mind along with spirit. You need to concentrate on improving your life all along the way. Do not wait until you are at death's door to decide you have not lived as you wished. Work along the way and get your house in order as you go. Whatever you do, do it well so you never have to do it over.

What is the proper philosophy of life?

If you visit a foreign capital, do you see all you came to see or merely skim the surface of the city? If you really see all you planned to see, you know you do not have to come back again. If you skim only the surface, you will want to return. Make sure you cover everything the first time. If you must return, you will know the terrain and how to get around the area more easily. The same principle applies to this life.

When neither alive nor dead, where are you?

We hear you asking such questions constantly, but you never wait to hear the answer. We want you to know this is not the only world you created. You have created a series of worlds. This is the only world you concentrate on while here, but you have access to others. The other worlds are not as developed, but you can and do go into them. What you often believe to be a dream is actually an episode wherein you enter another world and proceed to get so deeply involved you forget to close it when you return to this life.

If all this sounds confusing, you cannot follow what we have to teach you now. If you cannot follow us, you should ask for clarification. This requires you to shut down your senses and mentally ask for the clarity of inner control necessary to see what is meant—before attempting to read more material here....

If ready to continue, let us know by moving your mind ahead in time.

We are present as you read. Really! You may believe that only The Scribe knows who we are, but you know us, too. All people can tap into their inner sources. You are here on Earth and we are here also, but you are in flesh and we are not. So what?

The time to begin to understand another dimension is when you *know* it exists. If you do not understand that concept, you previously blocked all knowledge of dreams from your life. If you never used your dreams, you are lost now.

If you need to catch up with the class, remember your first day on Earth. How can you do that? We can do it. We can see every moment of your life here on Earth, but because it is of no value to your *mind*, you cannot. You need to know only the day you live in now and why you are here. If you know these two things, you can succeed. If you know why, it matters not when or where you were born—which is the dilemma.

Why are you here?

This is the most crucial decision you will ever make while on Earth. You have to know why you are here, but how do you find out? You might think it easier to travel backwards and relive past experiences until you arrive at the time of this birth, but that is '*past life regression*' and of no use to the future. You might decide to go forward in a dream or meditation, but that might not be wise, either. So how do you find out why you are here now? Ask!

If you want to know your purpose in life, sit down and ask about it aloud, then meditate until you know. The answer is there—within you. You only have to know to ask, then be willing to listen for the answer. Once you know all, it is so obvious!

You asked for help when you brought this life into being. Do you remember who you asked to help you? No, because you asked only You for help. Who are YOU? You are a multi-dimensional being with the ability to be several different beings at one time. You live on several different planes simultaneously and have the ability to know it. Why deny it? You do not wish to upset this world, because this world is a very fragile dream. If you question too much, it might disappear—really!

If this life is a dream, why not live in another dream? You can! You can live here or there. It matters not which dream, as long as you keep this body safe and sound and return to it at times. We see many of you enter other areas of the universe and return to this one, but you do not remember anything about it—like your birth on Earth. Death is the same, only you cannot return to the body then, because it no longer exists here.

We are aware you have much to think about in this session. We will let you go into deep meditation and remember all you can. If you forget anything, you can reread it easily. The same is true of your mind.

If you forget something, go back into your mind and retrieve it. You call this hypnosis, but it is mind control. Mind control or hypnosis is not of great use to you in this dimension, but it is of great use in others. If you learn how, you can use it often. We suggest you try it, and if it helps, use it. If you become confused, you are too susceptible to false clues and cannot enjoy control over the life you can command now.

You need to control your life...
Or it will control you!

This is the only order of the day not completed in this lesson: *What do you do if you cannot enter your body upon visiting another dimension?* We know it will not happen, but some people say it can happen. Why? Why would you believe you could enter another person's body or some other being could enter yours? It is simply not realistic! You have to rid yourself of such idle, weird thoughts, or be overtaken by them. Novelists are paid to be idle thinkers, but the average person cannot afford it.

Whatever you do, do it well and remember to live all these days your way. That is all there is to this life. If you do that, you cannot help but be ready to die—*which is the fear of your life while here.*

Once you can handle the fear of death, you are free of all it implies. No more phobias, idle worries, or deep depression for you. You live!

Chapter Eight

The time to be everything you ever wanted to be while on Earth is when you are here—not after you are gone. Please try to remember: *Our goal is to teach you how to successfully end your time on Earth and be able to ascend to the next plane at the end of this life episode.*

The work you do now is not work of the *devil* nor heavenly-inspired. You are doing your own work on this life and it reflects *you*. If your center (core of existence) is not as clear as it must be to return to the higher places within your being, you cannot make the leap when that time comes. If you can clear your center and have energy in reserve—no problem ever!

We seek to inform you of the days in which you will no longer be here or anywhere else on Earth, so we can help you—not scare you. If you gain access to new information, do you use it immediately or do you let it sit? The wise use whatever they can from whatever source they receive it, while the foolish sit and debate and scare themselves with the same facts. Are you wise or foolish?

The only people on Earth who are fully integrated are those who fear not death! If you still fear death, you cannot say you can transcend this plane. If your work is not as you would like it, when do you think it will be? Do you believe another will come and take you by the hand and lead you to your best life? If you think that way now, you will wait a long time.

The end of the world is not the end of all life, rather the beginning of a new and totally different life for those who choose to follow God. If you care nothing for the things you do—or have nothing to do, why would you think about doing something different? You must get busy to know why you cannot be as productive as you might be or as happy as you should be.

If you could change your life,
Would you?

Would you change this world into '*the end of all that we know*', as you say? Why? What good would it do you? You need only change you in order to affect change in your entire world. The world is not concrete, it is malleable—and you need only exert energy to change your space in it. Why would you expect others to change the world to suit you if you are unwilling to exert yourself and change it for them?

Be realistic in your condemnation of others and realize it is your world, too, and you have as much responsibility to change it as anyone else. Why change it is your worry, but how you change it is everyone's responsibility. It takes cooperation and painstaking attention to every detail to effectively change the entire process of living on Earth, and it takes time and effort to do this—nothing else!

The steps to take to effect change are not as difficult as those needed when you are not as easy in spirit and mind as you are now. You have come this far in our work together and continue to arrange your thoughts in patterns that accomplish much work while processing this information. This is how to go about your work and your life NOW!

You work and think at the same time!

Do not sit and stare at work—hoping others will do it. If you are prepared to work hard on this project daily and find only one other willing to work beside you, you will be further ahead when the time comes to ascend than all the millionaires alive today. You need not worry about who will clear the final hurdle—or why. You need only prepare yourself for it and help another. If each living person helped only one other cross to the next plane, the world could leap forward now.

You are never as you appear to others, and they seldom are as they appear to you, but so what? If you were transparent you would not have as many issues to work through as you do now. The issues which concern you this last life are the same issues you will use to protect you from those who will try to dissuade you from tackling the big problems—like destroying forests and plowing land for no lasting benefit to man and Earth.

The only issue of real worth to you is the one that worries you. If you have no worries now, you are ready to work for the good of all. We will help everyone clear their worries of the past in order to be productive the entire time each of you is on Earth.

Put your list of needs on the table and let us work out a plan now for when you will be clear, centered, and able to ascend.

1. Lay your head on your hands and concentrate on how many people you know now. Do you know 6, 7, 11, 35, 50 people very well? If you are integrated, you know only one—you! Start now to see how much you can share of yourself with another without cutting into the vital areas of your personal growth. Do you have a sense of what is of vital interest to you—what you cannot lose or take for granted if you are to progress all your life? Once you have this information and are ready to begin, let us know.

2. Pull out a pencil and paper and list everything you do very, very well, then list those you do very well, those you do well, those you do not do well, etc., until you can determine how much you have to draw upon in times of deep despair. If you have done nothing very, very well, you have nothing to complete your circle if you should drop into deep despair. As soon as possible, plan to work on one special attribute and perfect it. *Do it right now!* If you need years to develop even one, you are not realistically trying to change now. You are wasting your life here. Change gradually, if you must, but change!

3. Visualize your life as a line extending out in front of you. Do you see a snag or doubled line anywhere? Replace such an area with a solid dark line, then renew your energy so it will not create difficulties for you if it should snap and hit you. Remember, if your life is on the right track, death is not difficult and not to be dreaded. You have to learn to stand alone and be able to function well all your life—not just when left alone. Once you can take care of this life adjustment to death, it never throws you off-track again. You can learn how to manage death without actually sustaining grief, but most do not.

4. Love is the key element of most humans' lives. They are unable to further themselves beyond a certain point until they have another person to share their life and believe in them. Why? If you have never discovered who you are and why you are, do you believe adding more people to your life will help? Not likely, but it can help you transcend Earth. Why? Because you need to help others to also live and be ready to move forward without intruding into their lives. This is the easiest way to help: Marry or adopt another and let them enter into your mind. This sharing is what brings success and peace.

5. You now need to pray for strength and guidance. Do you pray? Do you ask for all your needs? Do you expect your needs to be provided? We would not ask all these questions if the world were a better place for souls to develop. This wisdom would be obvious. But now you need to pray for help, in addition to meeting your own needs. Ask for help and guidance and The Holy Spirit of God is there! You need only clear your mind and center your spirit to make contact. Once you make contact, your life is fully growth-oriented and happiness is yours, if you so desire. Why would you not desire it? It is your birthright to do what you want with this life.

6. Lastly, you need to listen to hear what God has in store for you and how you are to go about assuring your personal happiness. How do you do this? We continually ask you to meditate, but some are still resistant. Why? '*It is not easy,*' is the answer. If you are lazy or negligent—and you may be, if you do not meditate—why would you expect others to work and clear up your problems? This is not the way to live, and it is never respected. You must live your life knowing the only way to connect with God is in deep meditation or contemplation of your soul. Try it NOW!

This is not a sermon or a diatribe to get you out of a depressive episode. You have nothing to be depressed about now. You have a life which is yours to live, and if it gets out of balance as it does in depression, you have the means to reestablish its order once again. You are the only one who suffers when you get depressed. Why would anyone else be held responsible for causing it?

You need to offer up ideas on ways you think your life could be better and how you can do a better job on it, before it is given clearance for growth by those above *you*. Yes, there are higher planes, but you do not have concrete notions about who does such work—because you know nothing about them.

Let the hierarchy of angels go for now!

Get your life in order before calling upon those who are of God to help you do your work. To believe in God entails nothing, because you already believe in God! If you establish a hierarchy of beings to confront each time you approach God, you are who built such an empire in your mind that confronts God and is unsuitable for individual growth. Never place any being between you and God! You must realize you are of God, and God exists in you as much as God exists in others. Why would you believe an angel is higher than You?

We would like you to see the world as it is *before* you settle on how you can change it to become safer for others to grow and adopt godly ways, but seeing the world is not a travelogue. You need stay only in your safe place to '*see*' all there is to it. If you go out into the actual world of today, you will find confirmation of what you think it is. Therefore, it is a waste of time to go and check out your beliefs if you never previously studied the beliefs of others.

You cannot enjoy anyone else if you do not like yourself. If you are to take on the world, you must be okay with *you*. If your life appears to fit you now, proceed to the next problem. Once a problem is successfully resolved, you never have to go back to it again; but if you slide by—ignoring important aspects of a problem, it will return again and again until you do all the work required to solve it. Why not do that the first time around?

These are times the ancients wrote about. So what? Why be interested in what they said? You have only today to do your work and dwelling on warnings and superstitions left from the past wastes the present. You need to develop your life and get onto The Way of God—only then are you able to be *you*.

We will help you! Others of the higher planes are always around watching to see if anyone shows promise here. Why not surprise yourself and ask for help to define your life NOW? If nothing happens, so what? If you are successful and help arrives by the legions, what can you say then? We know of no one among the many now trying to develop who cannot reach the next plane at the end of this life on Earth.

Why do you doubt? You think rather than believe! Using the mind to do spiritual work is of little use to *you*, but The Holy Spirit can use the mind and adapt its workings for its use. The body is separate, as well as the mind. Spirit is the soul of your being and essential, but not your mind nor your body. If either the mind or body betrays you, it is not a big problem in the entire scheme of things, but if you betray your spirit, *you* will end.

Why not be safe now? Why not hedge your bets? Why not accept the eventuality that God is within you working now to save you trouble later? Why not try to develop a suitable philosophy that always works for you? If others adopted philosophies that comfort you, take what you like from theirs while developing what you need. It is not required that you tailor an entire philosophy, but it is necessary to adapt one to suit *you*.

Why would you need a personal philosophy? Because you are not a physical being with nothing within but muscle and blood, nor are you a rational-thinking machine. You are a complex being who chose to enter this Earth's atmosphere in order to further the growth of your entire being. It is not an easy lesson, but not the most difficult one, either.

Place your work for all to see, then watch others to learn if you lack anything. The world is not here to humiliate or sustain you, but you are to remain humble and accept God's good and not hinder anyone else from gathering all they need. If you try to stop others from gaining all they need, your needs will not be met!

You need only enough to live on and thrive, but some have huge appetites. An appetite of little use to you is the appetite for money. Think of all you have now and all you wish to have, do you really need more?

Greed in this life is the worst fear you placed before you now—and too many of your world flounder on it. Why? You scare yourselves. You do not know why you must have *things*, but you must!

You cannot remember what you had when a child, but are sure you have more now. What could misconstrue all this into a need to have every toy, game, and amusement known to mankind? Your mind! You are who demands such things. You are who sees and wants toys, games, and amusement. No one else cares if you have much—really!

The life of wealth which interests most is one where the individual personifies greatness as well. If you steal or rob others of their wealth, you do not gain their personas. In fact, you lose so much that others hate you—which is not why you came to Earth.

You all came to help and live as a cooperative association of people trying to improve yourselves spiritually. The reason you establish such elegant facades and develop such devious excursions in life has fallen by the wayside. Only winners avoid them. The losers of this life get hung-up in the byways and alleys constructed in this world to build character.

If your life is not over once you leave the world, why would you care what happened to your body? That is an ancient preoccupation which does not fit in with today's population, but there to be dealt with now. You can preserve your body, but why? Why would you want it? Did you ever *really* use a pressed flower you tucked away in a book to preserve its memory? No way can you use this body once you are gone, so its preservation is a waste of effort once you no longer live, but all the time you are on Earth you should preserve your body.

We end this segment on this note: You have never been counseled by anyone disinterested in you, but you often sought counsel from those unqualified to help you. Why? You do not trust *you*. Trust God and never worry again!

Chapter Nine

The only one not of Earth is the one on another plane. We are not of Earth, we are on another plane. What does *plane* mean? It means a different structure from this one—where there is no time.

You have enough time on Earth to do all you came here to do, but some never finish what they came to do. Why? They believe you will live forever. This belief is ingrained in *you*. It is true, but not as you understand it to be while on Earth. You do not live forever on Earth! You have only enough time here to do what has to be done, and then you go off to the next phase of life, which may not be on Earth.

What happens if you do not finish your work? You have to come back and do it, plus get more work. If you never finish anything, that can add up over a few lifetimes. So finish your work first, then play, study, or do whatever you like. If you put off doing your work, you may end up on Earth when the time comes that no human life can be sustained here—which would be a disaster you could have avoided.

Disasters are caused by people!

God does not plan to hurt anyone, but people become cruel and disinterested in others and let things mount up that can and should be corrected. You, by yourself, caused most of your problems, yet you have little patience with others who cause their own problems. Why? If you do not want others pointing out your errors, do not point out their errors.

If you get caught in an earthquake, do you blame God? You should not! Earthquakes are a phenomenon of nature that clear the Earth. If you build on solid ground, you are not in the path of an earthquake. Greed and mismanagement cause people to build and then live on shaky ground.

Do not blame God!

If you live near a forest, you can expect fires. God cleanses the forest of old-and-young trees from time-to-time to insure the growth of the middle range. You do not see God take away young or old people. That is something you all do. Forget blaming God for your troubles and you will be half-way to salvation. The other half comes when you learn to trust God.

The only time to forget about your work is when you are needed by another. It should not take long to help someone else. If it does, you are doing their work and should stop. All people need assistance from time-to-time, but you cannot do others' work for them. It would ruin them. Plan to help out if you can, but leave time daily to do your work.

The only time to remove work and not do it is when you cannot do it. If you set it aside, do it later when ideas flow and energy returns. This is both effective and efficient, but do not completely forget such work or it will return when most inconvenient to finish it.

The work of your day is not the work of night. You learn much at night as you sleep; and if you do not sleep at night, you learn less. You must be devoted to the work of this life if it is not to be repeated. If dreams are never recorded or watched to see if they hold meaning, how can you learn? You do, but such work has to be repeated and repeated, so sit down and learn it well once and be done with it.

Dreams are timesavers!

Dreams can help you sort through problems, understand people, as well as establish priorities, itineraries, and begin new projects. You are stupid to avoid the responsibility of writing your dreams down and trying to figure out what they mean. We have heard many people boast that they never dream. How foolish they sound to all others. Everyone dreams—period! The only time you do not dream is when over-drugged or on the edge of madness, otherwise, you dream a lot.

In the beginning of this life you decided to be a little less than what you could be, so there would be time to finish all you came here to do. If you are capable of more spiritual work, why do you do so little? Laziness—and you cannot disguise it. It is there for all to see. Only you think you can avoid work and no one will notice it.

All notice your efforts! There are times when you think others might not believe you are working, but that is not the same as others not seeing anything productive issuing from your life here. If you have any doubts now, *you* will know.

The only time to sit and do nothing is when you are relaxing or meditating, otherwise, do something with your hands whenever you sit and wish to relax. The hands are the means by which the brain is alerted to activity. If your hands are busy, the mind relaxes and lets the body do its work. If your hands are idle, the mind becomes exceedingly anxious trying to produce activity. If you go into a deep somnolence, the mind gets edgy and produces pictures and other stimulation to get you to move. If you let it, the mind will control your entire life here.

Some think the mind should control life,
But it cannot!

The mind is not in charge! It is the means by which you accomplish most of your life's desires, but it does not achieve or actually prepare your life goals. The Holy Spirit is a force within *you* that achieves and develops the life of each person on Earth. If an individual's spirit is harmed or deterred from being free, it equals imprisonment of the body, but few think of it that way.

Your mind, body, and spirit must be free if you are to know freedom, but most of you do not care about freedom now. Freedom is not something you value. Although it has no basis in reality for most, you fear false imprisonment, but little else. This is a major fear and a real concern for those who dwell in regions where false idols are still worshipped.

You may believe you worship God, but may not. How can that be? You never speak of God. You never set aside time or money to dedicate yourself to Good or God. You speak of yourself more than the power within *you* that does all that you brag about now.

How do you know God? You think. You study. You worship in a quiet place. You believe! You do not envy others or sink to levels beneath the one where you are now, or ask for what others possess. The rules are itemized by every major religion. Find a religion that suits you and follow it, if you have neither the time nor inclination to do all that work.

You can worship God alone. You can love all of God's work alone. You can be alone all of your life and let others live alone. If your loneliness drives you to gossip or conceit, you stretch the truth. If your loneliness is such that it destroys you, you hate. If you cannot talk to anyone, how do you sound now? How do you speak of your beliefs? How do you know who you are? You can live this life alone, but it is easier with friends.

Now that we are here and talking about friends, how often do you take time to be with them? If you say often, fine—but do you finish your work, too? No? Then you spend too much time with friends and not enough time with you. Friends will fill up your life if you let them, so adjust your schedule until your life is in balance.

The only one you need is *you*, but others help you ease through this time from birth-to-death, too. Anytime you find a wise and loyal friend is a time of great celebration. You must honor and keep all such friends, but remove all others as they betray their motives along the way. Continue to strive to be truthful, deliberate, and helpful! If you cannot find a friend, you live in the wrong area—move!

Now that you have a motive for finding a spiritual friend, will you? Will you seek out another to help you understand God? Such help is not available. You can find others who will worship with you, but they cannot worship for you, nor can you help them find God.

The only time to ignore your life is when you have it all in order and are on the right track. If your life is a little bit out-of-order or not headed in the right direction, all attention must be directed to it until it is corrected. We caution all who think they have their lives in order to watch carefully and seek out others then, because such faith is not to be wasted on self if not warranted.

If you work steadily, you have a lot of experience; but if you are often at ease and not busy, you have not yet observed all the areas in which you have much work to do now. Do not be harsh in your criticism, but examine your life more closely than others.

In the valleys of Earth are deep, deep crevices covered with tons of earth and water—so much so that they appear solid. You, too, have many valleys of spirit and thought that are cracks in your façade. If you sense anyone getting too close to your truth, you extinguish their interest or drive them away. If you drive away everyone you meet, you indeed have a lot of work to do. You have to delve deeply into *you* and figure out why you dislike or mistrust everyone you know. If there is a sound reason for doing so—move.

Why move if you can sit still? Movement sets up each day for the crisis or success guaranteed to happen. If you never move, you will never move up in the world. No one else will do anything for you! They may work for you as an employee, but you have to do your own work on self.

You cannot hire another to do your work of spirit. Your character is built by you, not someone else. How else could you live now?

In some localities there are people who thrive and those who do not. Why? Those who thrive, manipulate the environment in their own way. Many are not as capable as workmen who repair facades of buildings or remodel interiors and some are not as able to treat mental illness or physical pain, yet you all need these skills to have a full life. You, too, must adapt to the environment or move.

You always have a choice!

You do not need others, but they are part of your plan. Sit down and let others do your work and you will quickly see their work is not what you want. If others work for you, let them do a job correctly their way or get rid of them. Never direct workers from over their shoulders or criticize them for not seeing things as you do.

No two humans' eyes are the same. You may think others see things as you do, but they do not. Your eyes perceive life as you color it. If you see things in a dim light, you see only obscured colors and shapes. If you stand in the light, you look brighter and see things in a different light than those who remain in the shadows. Occasionally look at life from different directions so you can tell where it might be better for you at that particular time. Some crave the shade, others the full sun, whichever is not important because you need both.

Your life never appears as big as others, because you stand behind it—not in front of it. Look in a mirror and view yourself. Do you command too much attention? Are you too brilliant for the rest of the cast? Are you silly? Do you weep a lot and act like life is a constant pain? You are an actor and can emote or not, but why blow up the scene more than it needs to be if you plan to only be here a short time?

In the world of business are many actors and actresses of great ability. You meet them every day and laugh or cry as you are prone to do, knowing they are playing a part, too. Why get so involved in a play you cannot appreciate its meaning? To appreciate it fully, you need to back off and look at the entire scene. If you stand too close or wait in the outer lobby until it is over, you never know why you came to the play or what is happening on stage now. Enjoy life as a play! If you like to cry, make your life a drama. If you like to laugh, make it a comedy. After all, you can rewrite your life story as you rehearse it.

For some, there are many times when hardship intrudes directly into their lives, but that seldom is the case for the general population. Why? Some people have decided to make this their last life on Earth, but have a lot of unfinished business from the past to attend to now, thus they overload themselves with challenges. However, if they can make it this life, they are winners for all time!

If you chose to live out a deep, depressive winter in a land of no trees, why would you say God almost killed you last winter? The land is as it is. You can move, but the land stays. Take your camp elsewhere. Move with the sun or move away from the sun. Enjoy freedom, but never blame God if the home you left is gone when you return.

Some of life's treasures cannot be taken from you, but some things you work for now can and will be stolen. You cannot expect others to know how precious things are if you are careless with them. Many people mistreat animals—even humans, and expect them to remain loyal. How absurd is that?

Do not remain anywhere you are not wanted. If you are to be happy, leave the old and quickly adopt the new practices of the new location. The only ties to remain from the old place are the ones you wish to keep. Drop all others as they will not help you adjust to a new level of living.

Every time you relocate you move up or down—never lateral, so be sure you are going in the right direction now. Sometimes you can save time and energy by moving back to where you started, but seldom are you welcome if you do. Be sure you have a welcome mat out to others now, if you expect to use them in the future. The only welcome guests are generous hosts!

If your life is so difficult that you cannot stand to be in it any longer, you made it that way and can change it. Sit down and meditate, then rethink the way it got this way and how to change it—visualize yourself living in the new way. It is easy, but seen as a miracle by all who do not know how God works today.

When your time to be of service to others is over, relax and enjoy this time! Why put off your work schedule if you are not going to do work you enjoy? Begin each day and end it doing something for you, but you do not need to do big things to enjoy life. Be careful of escalating the stimulation required to be pleased. It can become a burden!

If your life is growing into the area of life where breaches of contract occur (such as divorce), and no one likes your decisions, sit down and think about each decision before actually making a move. You can move, but you pay heavily for hasty ones. We suggest you decide what exactly you dislike, then attempt to repair it.

If you cannot repair a relationship, house, garden or whatever, you need to seek a replacement, but do not let the one you have go without much thought. Seek out help and decide whether or not the replacement is any better than what you have—then decide before you move. This is very obvious, yet now the most common practice in your societies relative to failure with relationships is to replace all you know and enjoy with something unknown.

If you think of another as being you, do you think they think as you do? If so, you are not thinking of them! You are merely transferring your motives to them, thus cannot understand them. We suggest you believe you are the other for a few seconds and see what comes to you. If you sense a determination not to like you, then you do not like them. If you sense a mean streak or malice, it is you being mean; but if you sense a strong love coming from your first impressions, be nice to whomever and realize they do not know you, but could become friends. If you strongly dislike them, it is your decision as to what you intend to do about it—not theirs.

Why would you want to be someone else? We see too much jealousy and envy in the world, yet there is so little separating each of you from all others. How would you be *you* if you had to be exactly like someone else; and why would you want to be exactly like someone else now?

You need time to review all this material. We cannot spend time, because we do not recognize its existence, but you do. If your idea of spending time thinking is not the same as ours, can it be the same as anyone else's idea? No, your sense of time is yours alone. You never have to stay awake for another or go to sleep for someone else. You need to do it for *you*. The plain and simple truth of life is that you do everything as you wish—and you do it when you want to do it!

Chapter Ten

This is the time to begin taking stock of your life and letting others do the same. If you spend time working on others, you let your work go—and who will do it for you? You need to always finish your work first!

Work is the theme of this session on time and the two go together in your world. You have nothing you must do but spiritual work! So work at it all the time and when you get to the point where your work of this life is done—then help others.

If your work is not as easy as it appears to be, you can realize the same is true for everyone else, too. All work if done well appears easy! Only the immature think others have less work. You must always be alert for anything that looks like you have less work than someone else. If that ever happens, you are then flirting with laziness. Your work should leave you no time to watch others work.

Others who fill your space are not as active or are more active than you are. It is a fact and not hard to see, but some always try to do less or more than other people. Why? If you do your spiritual work, who cares if the rest do their work?

In the final analysis of this life, all who live on Earth are viewed as being of the same race. No one outside of Earth sees any difference. You all look alike! So why not act like you see each other as being in the same race? It would easily eliminate a lot of friction. Friction is what tears at the fabric of a nation and your world. To let racial tension enter into a nation is to permit anarchy—and it destroys peace.

If anarchy is permitted to ruin a country, it will. It is the unruly mobs of history who prevented life from surging forward. The mob intellect is not one of niceness or gentility. It is low-born and crass. It is not of great intellect or usefulness. You must make sure the mobs are instructed in the ways of God or you could end up with nothing. Mobs are lazy. They take. They kill. They steal. It matters not the race, creed, or nationality—mobs are not good for mankind.

What we like to see are small cooperative groups or tribes working to better themselves. If they do that and have money, crops, or even time left over to help others, they should share it. If a tribe has not enough for itself, it means it is not effectively managed or efficient. A new leader is needed then—not more territory.

In some countries there are many tribes that do not agree. It becomes a matter of politics to be on top—to be in control. This tribal warfare is not conducive to growth and can produce anarchy. Mobs will decide what leaders do not!

You have to form productive enterprises that encourage each member to do something for themselves while taking care of the major goals of the group. If you do not, they will feel alienated and end up in a mob. The word '*mobster*' is used by some to refer to a person who breaks the law, but it means a person who is unruly and irrational. To break laws is not a reliable way to live. You have to have rules to determine which direction all will drive and where houses are safe from industry, but to rule every aspect of life invites anarchy.

You should overhaul your legal system NOW!

The only peace you will know while on Earth is the peace of being one with God. No other peace prevails. Warriors shed their armor only to reinvent another war. You have to live in God to appreciate peace. If you let your heart go to war, you will never be at peace. If you are at peace, but war appears necessary, you will not be of any worse disposition after the war than you were before; but if you let others rule your life because you lack ambition and confidence, a war can ruin your peace.

In the work of the world are many who live to war. They love it! They would rather fight with someone than work beside them. These people fill the workplace today, and as a result work is not getting done. Why? You decide! You are of the world and you decide who runs your home, industries, and whatever else you deem necessary for progress.

Why do you condone idle, negative behavior from public officials and big institutions? You do not care! If you pay high tariffs for utilities and do not know why, you are condoning the way they operate. The public should pay little or nothing for utilities, because they are of the Earth and require very little to turn on or off—and all need them. To make a competition out of such business is to condone the use of graft to get what you need to live.

Whatever you do, do it as though you can live without it—but remember it is best to do it now. This spirit of enjoyment is always present if you look at the overall job. You may not like the habits and attitudes of those who work with you, but does the job get done? That is the test. If you are at fault, correct it immediately. If someone you work with is at fault, it is the supervisor's responsibility to see it is corrected—not yours. Be aware you, too, look irresponsible to others at times.

You may look like a leader when you hold public office, but seldom are public officials real leaders. Public officials take orders and are not permitted to be of use to you personally. If they take orders from you, they no longer serve The Public. To demand personal service from public officials is corrupt. Public officials are not corrupt, but those asking for favors are. Be aware of the part you play in corruption.

If your life is filled with wares you did not purchase, or you helped others steal from another, you are a thief. No wonder you all steal, you all have huge appetites. If you stopped to watch even one bird, you would see it eats all it finds. It does not store it or ask another to take care of it. If times are bad, humans may pitch in and help them, but mostly God takes care of the birds, and they are fully aware of it.

If you are to get to the next plane you need less and less—rather than more and more. The life you live now is not the life of your eternal soul. Far from it! Even now more life is found on another plane than you have on Earth.

Why burden yourself with so much junk? Whatever you do to better this world helps you. If you do nothing, your life is diminished. You do not think others will give their work to you—do you? Why? If your family taught you to take all you can get, and everyone else was taught the same thing, how would any of you create anything to steal? You would not.

You are either a thief—or not!

Thieves make up the bottom stratum of any society. If you live in an area rundown or poor, you know thievery is the reason. You watch someone take from another and sell it—and you buy. If all refused to buy, thieves would not steal. So if you buy from a thief, you are one, too. Do not think there is a difference!

Whatever stratum of society you live in now, remember to live. You cannot live well if you owe everything you make or need everything you see. To be so greedy that you owe all you have to others is to be sinfully rich. You are never going to get all you want! That is a fact of life.

If you are never satisfied, you will work more. If dissatisfied for a long time, you would eventually fold your tents and leave the area. You need the satisfaction that comes from conquering doubt and delving into new territory. Land is the physical manifestation of territory, but it is not the territory you need to explore now.

You need to explore your spirit NOW!

You have so much unseen work to do, and so many places to travel, it is inconceivable you will do even one-half of it before leaving Earth. To go on to the next plane requires a degree of proficiency in spiritual matters. You have to know things which can only be learned through The Holy Spirit. Your mind is empty of anything that cannot be determined by the eye or heard by the ear, but your spirit can take in everything!

We would never ask anyone to work constantly—never able to rest, but you often do it to yourself. You need rest to do your best work! If you are resting and someone approaches you to begin work, tell them you will do it—but continue to rest. If the one wishing you to work continues to hound you, reevaluate their position in your mind. If such a person is unworthy of you, do not worry.

You never work for those who are of no use to you. You work only for those who are of use to the furtherance of your life, so get your mind straight on that now. If you ignore the foreman, you could lose your job, but if you ignore the company clown, you may not. Some people do not understand to whom they owe their living and who does not deserve their time. Make sure you understand the difference.

If your life is not your own—why? Why would you work for someone else? Slaves are never slaves of spirit—only of body. Your mind forces you to accept roles. It enslaves you. If your body is not enslaving you but your mind is, why do you work only on intellectual matters? You need to free the mind. You need to cause it to back down and let you live.

If your mind never rests, you cannot physically rest, either. The body is overrun by commands from the mind and ends up overproducing acid or other corrosive materials that can eat away at vital tissue. Do not let your mind run your life!

In a spiritual life, all is welcome. In a mental life, all is examined and cast aside if unknown. In a physical life, all is wasted that is not used immediately. Which life explains you?

Do you know you? Why not? Why are you resistant to spiritual growth? Why do you think '*the devil*' is after you? You are no one without God! God exists and you are part of God, but '*the devil*' is a figment of overactive minds.

The spiritual work you do is for you. You do not work for *'the devil'* or any other being. You do it for YOU. If you doubt that, listen to the area within your mind that dictates your actions. What are you being told to do? Do you do all that your mind tells you to do? No, you cannot. The mind is constantly dreaming of ways to end your rest. You never rest if your mind is in control, so let up on thinking a lot.

Relaxation is the key to growth!

If you ease up long enough to let whatever is old drift away so what is new gets a foothold, you will gain more time through relaxation than by working straight through the day. It is inefficient to constantly work physically. The most productive workers are those who stop, rest, and think about the next step—before doing it. You need to direct your mind, not let it rule you.

Whatever you see or do is not for you alone. It helps others as well, but is primarily the cement that holds the universe together. You are only one being among countless legions, but if you do your part and every other being does its part, all are working for The Universe. If you do your work on Earth, *The Universe* is the only insurance you ever need.

The time to begin working on you is whenever you start doing something of a useful nature. If your work is not useful, why do it? To do something just to make money will end with you losing it. Sometimes you lose money, but you do not necessarily lose *you*. You may even find yourself then.

If the work of your day is even half as big as you are, you have enough time to do it all. If your work is too big for you, you will never get it all done, so let it go. You need to work on what suits you now. If you take on too huge a task, you will end up disgruntled or out of sorts with everyone else. Use sense and lose ego along the way and all is yours!

Whatever you do here, the ego is in charge. You need the ego to tell the body what to do, but you do not need it. You have a lot of time on Earth when you are not in your right mind, yet the ego takes care to see all your duties completed. You can wait until later to take care of some things, but bodily functions require constant use and care. The ego takes care to see that the body gets fed, cleansed, and other necessary details so the body can continue to function. You do not need to worry about the body if the ego takes care of its needs.

What if you and your ego are not on the same wave length—which is common? You fear everyone you meet. You gain weight and do not know why. You eat food to be full, but do not care if the body can use it or not. You eat nothing of worth to the body. You do not care to exercise. You do not want food, water, or exercise to interfere with work. Your work becomes so dominant you have nothing else in your life. The condition known as '*workaholism*' is not a disease of the body, it is a *dis-ease* within the mind.

You must control your mind NOW!

What if your body and spirit are not on the same wave length? You will not notice much. You will be without strength of character and unable to decide much of anything. You will be prone to depression. You will eat and sleep too much. You will not let others enter your life. You cannot let the body rule you. The body has no sense.

If your spirit is in charge, you function on all levels. You are in top form then. You can know when the mind needs a break, when the body needs food or rest, when the ideal time to do anything has arrived. The only way to live is to live in spirit NOW!

What if you died right now? What would happen? Not much! Your body would slump and all functions stop. Your mind would be unable to control you, and you would slip out of the body and arrive at the upper limits of this plane where you would stop. Once your spirit is free of the body it can observe what is going on and why, but will not be told anything until you cross over to the next plane.

When a body dies, it creates no problem. It enters a state of putrefaction and all goes back to its origin. No big deal! Your body is not a temple. It cannot be used again. You do not take care of it for the next life—you take care of it for this one!

When the mind sees the body is gone, it is free to flee. You never see the mind. It disappears! It has no further use to you, and it is not of use to anyone else, either. The mind disappears!

What you see in the ether is not your mind but spirit. If you can see it, you will notice it appears as a very light color or substance. It is not powerful and has no ability to intrude upon anything else. How can something like that come back and take over another's life? Be realistic—it cannot!

If all your friends can see something, can they see it for you, too? No, you have to see things your way. If it takes you longer, you may remember the experience far better. If it takes less time for you to see things, learn to be tolerant of those who are slow to admit anything into their consciousness, because they are then helping you admit more into yours.

Whatever you do, work hard. Whatever you want, ask for it. Whatever you need, you will get it. It is not hard to work if you know why you are doing it. It is the indecision of the mind that controls your level of satisfaction—not The Holy Spirit. If you are spiritually well-adjusted, your life is in tune, too. Be sure you know *you*—then all is well.

With only one other area of work unattended to here, we cannot leave this subject for all time without saying you need to work on your spiritual nature. If you have nothing of spirit to do now, how do you think your life will be in the future? It will be hopeless! You need to be *you*, and you need to know this life is your life. If you get all this straight now, you will never work in vain again.

Life is for the worker. If you do not work in spirit, you will not live. Be sure of what you want and it is yours. Be afraid of anyone, and they will have power over you. Do not envy anyone anything and you will have everything. Life is really that simple!

Chapter Eleven

Your life is not over when you *cross over to the other side*. It merely reveals itself to the upper planes while actively being described by actors of this life as a terrible time for them—but the best of times for you!

No one dies! You merely transform into the next stage of development. If your life on Earth was one in which all your goals were accomplished and you harmed no one getting them done, you will be examined and tested to determine if you learned what you set out to learn, then you are free to examine the next plane and determine where you will fit in best there. It is a time of evaluation and the best of all times for *you* to be alive here and now.

Each stage of life is dramatic, but the next stage is the most difficult, because anyone living on Earth is determined to stay here. Why? You think you are dead once you leave Earth. It is the sorriest of states to be in, but it lasts only as long as you believe it. Would you prefer to remain in a state of suspended animation forever? If you choose to stay on Earth always, you will.

Stay away from the darkness of Earth and you have an excellent chance of emerging into the light at the end of this transit. Because we have no worries about our existence, we cannot quite comprehend the fear and dread most people develop while living on Earth. Why would you want to stay here? It is no longer a beautiful planet. Wherever you go there are trashy scenes and crowded conditions. Whatever you do, you have to fight for space, and whatever you do is never done alone.

We are not as interested in you right now as you are in us, but we are assigned to this job and do it willingly. We have to work—just as you do! We do not offer ourselves up for sale, but are required to work. All creatures have to work.

When you sit down and look at the sky, do you see anyone on the way down? No! That is because you cannot see anything but other human beings. If you could see as others do, you would know you are not alone. We could count angels on a pinhead, but why do it? The *'number of angels on a pinhead'* theory is silly because it makes the mightiest of heaven seem insignificant. We caution anyone from making that mistake. It could be deadly!

If your life is not going along well now, you may see it as being the fault of someone else, but it rarely is. Usually it is you who have let others take control of your life. If you do that, you lose.

You are held totally responsible for the life you live here on Earth. There are no excuses allowed. When your life on Earth is done and you are busy with plans for the next stage, you will know that all you did on Earth served you—not someone else, otherwise it was of no use to you.

We welcome your compliments!

We are no different from others working in the upper planes, but some of you constantly compliment the wrong people or beings now. Why? Are you so ignorant of who does what that you cannot perceive angels are not archangels, saints, or otherwise different from you? You must learn that now.

If your life on Earth grows bigger and bigger and bigger every year, you begin to believe you made it happen. We loathe and detest the boasters, but you can boast. We cannot stop you! You can boast and get it all over with now, because later it is not a good idea. On the next plane you cannot call attention to yourself. It is not good form.

You are to conduct yourself as though God is within all your work. This is hard for too many humans to comprehend today, thus they will have to return. If you return to Earth for another life, you may be unable to avoid the end of this planet. If you have to be here then, it could be very miserable.

We strongly urge you to be better-mannered and always appreciate what God does for you. The best way to express yourself to others is to silently repeat the following prayer while in front of a mirror and looking deeply into your eyes:

> *'I am a child of God. I am delightful in every way. I seek the life of God and am prepared to die. I love Earth and all it is, but I must leave it one day.'*

If you silently say this prayer over and over again, you will reprogram and connect your inner life to your goal while here. If you refuse to reprogram your mind, your life will be spent in a series of mishaps—until one day you die and have no one to blame but yourself for not reprogramming your mind. It is not a secret that all the lives you lived are within your mind, but the mind is not the depository of future lives—the soul is.

We suggest you encourage your mind to seek out its own rewards and let you work within Spirit now. If your mind is not on your side, it is against you. However, you believe your mind cannot be against you. The truth is—you are not a combination of body, mind, and spirit. You are in control of each part, but only your Spirit is you.

If you expect to die, get ready for the end. If you die before you are ready, what then? We expect to now be able to help some of you understand more about that process so you can be all you came here to be and get on with your life when this segment ends.

What you need now is a part to play that helps you advance. If you live a life of idleness, you will not move up. If you live a life of total intolerance of people unlike you, you learn too late the difficult lesson that all people are the same to God. You will then be unable to do much about any evil you committed so far; however, evil can be eliminated by a life of good work now or in another life.

In the beginning of each life there is a period when all are asked to believe in God. Each soul reaffirms this belief. However, shortly thereafter a new and deeper conviction takes place—that you are human. You begin to believe in that being more than you believe in God. Remember, it is a trap! If you cannot end your asylum on Earth, you will be here forever.

Put your life on hold and make your mind stop caring so much about why you are here and instead decide to be *you*. If you learn nothing else from us—let it be that you must be *you*! If we can teach you that simple idea, we will become the best of all teachers. We hope you get the point!

What if you were *you* and everybody laughed at you? What would it do to *you?* Nothing! You are laughed at when not being yourself, so why be upset by being laughed at for being *you?*

It is not the work of God that upsets you, but the work of man. You do not like to work for others, but you must work. We suggest you learn a trade, but most of you aspire to manage others, because you believe it pays more and has higher prestige among other humans. We disagree.

You need time to become *you,* and time is why we are here. You have structured your life to become a place where time is the preferred method of challenging everyone to be in good form. If anyone is late, you call them to task. If anyone cares not for this system, you usually ostracize the person or group; however, they can be reinstated when they show proper respect for time. Tardiness is the number one reason people are fired. It is a fact of your life, so learn to handle time well now.

Your life on Earth is one of consensus. You have to live together and learn to become all *you* are, but to do this requires a lot of time. You have to live, retire, and die before you know life was very short. Your life here is not long, but it is eternal!

Why not live on another side of the Earth? Why live as you do now? You decided to live this way. You decided to settle where you are. You are not alien in your home, but elsewhere you may feel you are. When that happens, you leave less and less the home you built. Why live on Earth if you do not intend to be with others? You cannot end your life living alone or you will become all the many things you hate.

You have to develop into a loving personality, which takes at least one other to do it well. What you need to develop your life is one friend, but two or more make it easier and easier to live well. With each friend you increase your experience and gain time. Time is saved when a friend recommends something that works for you. If you listen to the advice of friends, you are spared making decisions. You have to leave Earth alone, so why not live together now?

Work is the best place to find friends, but it is not a good place for most who live in the West now. People at work are too competitive to make good friends. They cannot all hope to win, but all seek a prize. What is the trash of one life is a bonus for another, but how can it matter if you cannot leave Earth and are forced to live here when the end of time arrives?

The end of this world is not the end of time, but time is an integral part of this world. It is the structure that keeps all in sync. If you do not want to be in sync, you simply make sure you are always late. If you are late, you can object when told you are being insubordinate, but the bigger the gap—the bigger the lie. You cannot be late without lying. You have to tell the truth or let this life go. If you try to add up why you are late, you usually end up saying you did not want to be there—and that can get you into trouble—so say you could not get there any sooner and be done with it.

Why lie?

You lie to defend your ego. Why? The ego is not a culprit who does evil, but it is the perpetrator of all evil. While in spirit you cannot harm anyone else here, but the mind is capable of dreaming of evil which the body will complete.

If not careful, the spirit of *you* can become corrupted. The corruption of your spirit is not an offense against God, but ends your relationship to God. If you do not offend God, your life is one of goodness. If you offend God and it is not noticed while here on Earth, we can tell you now that it is noticed above—always. Better exchange a life quickly then, for you will be returning to Earth. The quicker you return the better!

What you do is not as important as how you do it. You know that, yet continually think you can change the natural order while here to suit the time you are in now. We suggest you not try to change the order of anything—but flow and grow with it.

When you object to anyone, or are upset about anything, you raise your blood pressure but not your social standing. You must learn to sit and relax and let time make its own way through your life. Once you sense it is time to act, never hesitate—do it NOW!

If you waste time, you know it, but seldom realize it if you save time. Why? Because you are not rational beings. You do not think in rational standards ever! You often tell others you are very rational, but no one is. We know you to be irrational, irritating, and ignorant, still we cannot change you. Only you can eliminate the ignorance that binds you to Earth.

If you see others not of your faith, do you ignore them? Probably, but you could learn much about your own faith if you tested it against theirs. If you believe, you believe! No one can change you. You, however, must realize you cannot change anyone else, either.

What you have is what you do. You do not need time to sit and think, but to sit quietly you need thoughts. Each day provides time to sit and stare at the ceiling, but not when you go to bed. Some of you cannot sleep because you did not use enough energy. Why?

Why eat or drink so much that it is sits in your stomach—not being burned for fuel? You do not want to sleep! You know you cannot eat and immediately go to bed. That is a fact, but over and over again you cannot grasp the information about fat. Who is dumb—you or your mind? The mind is not a dumb animal in charge of you, but you let it change *you*—which is dumb.

We challenge all of you to determine why you bought this book or borrowed it. You can say it was an impulsive action or you were inspired, but it was you who bought or borrowed this book. If you can do all things, why not do them well—and to be on the safe side, harm no one else?

The end of your life here is when you feel nothing. If death comes to you now, you might as well end your life quickly. We caution you from attempting to heal someone else of a problem if you are sick. If you try to heal another while ill, you can end your life. It is not easy to heal others, but it can be done. If your life is full of grief, then healing others appeals to you. You can heal all your sorrows by healing one other person, but you will most likely end up dead doing it when you are sick.

If your body cannot tolerate much love, you may hand your life over to someone who will give you much love and it will heal you; but if you cannot tolerate hate, you will not die if a hate-filled person enters your life, because you will become uncomfortable and leave—or should.

Why risk your life?

We understand why some people do that. Riches are often the reason some tolerate much abuse, but in the end such riches are not worth the time their lives are being soured and scarred, thus unable to accept anyone else's love for them.

You have now read about a number of theories regarding why you do what you do, plus a sprinkling of ideas and theories about your life on another plane, but you still do not know anything. You cannot know God, yet you claim to be able to determine which way you will grow today. You will never grow if you do not honor God. That is fact, so accept it now!

In the end of time there comes a place where you decide to let go of this life. We suggest you sit and relax now and enter into a meditative state in order to release all your fear of life, so you can end your fear of death. Once you do that, all of this life is filled with love.

This is a short session because life is full of surprises. You often need to sit and read a lot of material before you can digest its meaning, but you need only sit and read one book now to discover who you are. Why spend your time reading others' work? You are curious.

Why become interested in something, if it is of no interest? You are interested or you would not read or write about this subject. Admit you are you and life is easy. Deny who you are, and life is difficult.

The time to end a difficult chapter is not when the reader thinks it is difficult, but when the time to end it arrives. Life is the same. Let it end. Let it go. Let it flow away and end one day. Never stop the flow!

Chapter Twelve

Your life is your time! You do not have to work. You do not have to do anything here. But if you decide to idle, you will return to Earth until you decide to work.

If you decide to become a hermit, never associating with others, you will never learn to tolerate all people and will be returned. If you decide to become a big-time investor in others' money and then take their money, you will return. It is the way!

What you do is why you are here. If you do nothing, you will have to return again and again until you learn what you are here to learn. The big difference in classes is that some have very little to learn, while others are doing several lifetimes' work at once.

If your life is a great drama, you have decided to quickly do it all. If your life is an easy one, you may have decided to come back to finish up only small details, but it could be you are *not* working on you. The difference from one life to the next is so great that no two people resemble one another, so it is foolish to compare. You cannot get any acceptable data that way.

To explore a life in depth in order to understand the workings of the mind is a waste of energy. You can only find insights into one mind—yours. You cannot draw conclusions or compare your findings to others. If you do, you could harm someone else.

It is best to understand the basic premise of life: Do no harm to anyone—including you...then try to understand why you are who you are to others. Others see you in their dimension and from their perspective, but you see and know yourself from your core.

You cannot be helped by someone dropping by from time-to-time to chat, but you can help yourself if you talk. Talking aloud is the actual benefit of psychoanalytical sessions. If you talk aloud to *anyone*, it helps.

Why talk about problems?
It helps!

If you get to the bottom of a problem, it need never appear in your life again. If you are to remove anything from your life, you must understand why it crops up again and again. Some problems reappear in different guises, but merely shades of the same problem. Review your relationship with anyone who continues to haunt your thoughts. Ask yourself: *"Why is this person continuing to bother me,"* so you can find out. If you never ask, you will be bothered by it forever.

The person you were last year is not here this year. How could you change? You just do! It is a simple fact. If you are inclined to argue over simple facts, how do you accomplish anything? You do not! You need to stop and think over all you do before and after an event and realize you changed in the course of the event. That is all there is to know.

Once you know *you*, you have the world. The world is a microcosm of the universe, and you are a microcosm of this world. This world contains nothing that is not in you to a certain degree. It is up to you not someone else to magnify the positive and decimate the negative. If you change, you force others around you to change, and so on and on. It begins a cycle which is repeated. Change yourself first, then the world will change, too!

What you want is not necessarily good for you, but you will get it. If you ask to live the life of another personality, you will get it and may regret it, but you will get it. If you ask for the time of day, you will find someone who has a watch. If you ask for time, you never get it from others. You must watch your time while here!

If your life is not open to question, you cannot expect others to answer your questions. If you continually ask questions of others, you will be called upon to answer their questions. If questions are of little obvious use, why ask them? Because it is a way to draw attention away from yourself. If you get another to talk, you can design statements, redraw your position, or begin new work.

It is not a time to begin anything, but you usually try to begin things as you end work, which is unwise. If you wish to be done with a job forever, completely finish it before beginning the next one. If you drag your feet and do little planning on the next position, it may help more than if you advanced it a lot of energy.

Do not worry about falling *'behind'*. You are never behind. You always live as you go, thus impossible to get behind in life. It is merely a feeling or fear that you are missing out on life that makes you worry that you are falling behind. If you are enjoying yourself, you do not fear you are missing out on anything.

The only time to begin a new work is when the old work is done. If you try to start a new job before then, you cannot do it correctly. To experience a sense of completion, you must end the first job and let time take you to the next assignment.

To rush or fret is a problem—not of time, but self. You never have more or less time, but you have greater control or you do not. If you control your time and space, who can take it away from you? No one but *you*!

If your life is on the line and a deadline must be met, how do you do it? You make a firm commitment to be done on time. Give yourself extra leeway then, but it will be done. You need not fear missing the deadline. It will all be accomplished.

If you vacillate or otherwise delay, you earn demerits, but earning demerits indicates you can earn extra points. Why? You see yourself then as being overburdened or upset by the way *"God runs Earth,"* but you are totally wrong. You are not overburdened or upset by others—only by you!

You do not want to do extra work, because it might indicate your work on Earth is finished. You wish to stay on and on, because you are accustomed to Earth's atmosphere and think you can handle it. You cannot! You will know more about it later.

Why not earn extra points as you go along? It is easier that way, but requires time. Time is not of any use to us, but it certainly is of obvious use to you. If you ignore the concept, you become a slave to it. If you conquer it, you learned one of the lessons about why you came to Earth. For extra points, get busy working on time NOW!

What about time is so difficult to understand? We see philosophers conferring on the concept as though it were meritorious—and requiring deep thought, but it does not. It is—and it exists for you while here. You prepared a life based on the calendar—thus it exists.

You will not leave Earth until you understand why you came here—and the biggest lesson of all is TIME! Begin to study it NOW! Use it to your best advantage in order to be out of here at the end of this life. Refuse to learn how to keep time and you will be back again.

What if you learn all there is to know about time? We doubt you will, but if you do—teach others. You need to learn the concept first, then practice to demonstrate it exists and is at work now—then you can teach. What you teach is of little consequence if you know what you are talking about.

Teaching something you know nothing about is impossible. The Scribe was once asked by her superiors to teach a class on dreams, but she refused. She hired another who had *'better qualifications'*—at least on paper. During the course she learned her method of old was still within her. She could have easily taught the course but doubted what she knew. Why? She had no certificate of formally studying dreams this life, and thus doubted she knew enough to teach others. If we trust knowledge generated in the past and can teach it to others now, we can see this life has already been lived.

What if you called others to task about something you do not do yourself? Would you fear they would not want you? What would you fear? Why?

What could you do to anger anyone? You can ignore *you* and try to be someone else. That is the problem when others turn against you. You changed into someone they do not recognize. If always *you*, there is little change, your face remains recognizable even if your name or body changed. You save face by staying in the life you came here to live. You cannot lose face by following your path.

What if you have no path?

It is ridiculous to think you came here without a plan. Why would you go anywhere new to you without a map? To get lost? What is the point? You have to learn to trust your mind and body—and live within the scheme of this world, then do your thing.

Fully advance the work of this world before seeking another job. If you can succeed in the world, you can do well anywhere on Earth. It is the same medium, but differs from worlds away from Earth in so many ways that it can become a handicap to be worldly. Learn other ways, but remain in this world as you are today.

You may sense a difference when meditating, but it lasts only as long as you meditate. Why? It is not as though you were someone else, but it is difficult to explain to others that it is *you*. Why not let this become you all the time? You are here on Earth to be *you* and survive within the confinements of this plane—not live on another plane while here. Once you leave this plane you will live in another and another until all is known, but that takes forever.

You need to now learn to grow and develop, but need not do it today. If your life is not well-lived, you are penalized, you do not enjoy your time spent here. Enjoy yourself while you learn and do it well. If your life here duplicates old work, it is easier then, but it gets harder as you move into other areas.

Some lives are reversed. Some choose to do all their old work immediately, while others choose a carefree youth. It is up to you—really! You decide what you will do before you get here—but *you* decide. If your life is not as you see it to be, you think your eyes deceive you. It is not your eyes—but your mind. You need eyes to see and you need a mind. You are you regardless of any handicaps to those vessels.

You are who is—not your mind, body, or the eventual decline of either. If you find you cannot advance according to plan on Earth, you can ask for an extension of time. You must do what you came back to do!

Now you are all agog to hear about life after death. Why? You do not believe life is eternal!

If you accept the belief that life is a circle—and most say they do, you cannot comprehend life is over at the end of one segment. It is impossible to comprehend an idea and then not accept an action that proves it, but you do *not* comprehend this idea and you cannot accept a simple action proving it.

The Church of today is an empty one, but it will fill again as you decide to enter and change it to suit *you*. If you do not enter *The Church* and change it, you will have wasted one of the greatest achievements of your society. You left *The Church* as a child in order to grow into an adult. It is adults who return and restore *The Church*. If you do not, you let it decay and others rot. You will be unable to lay claim to helping this world if you let its greatest institution go now.

What you preach is not important! It is the nature of people to reject the advice of others anyway, but you all need time to sit and contemplate the work of your lives. A sermon often helps you identify the real problems you are experiencing this life. You need to form new congregations, but building new churches will not restore what once was. It is not a way of life now, but it can be.

If you wish to now enter the priesthood, you must put aside all the trappings of this world, but not in the future. You can be a priest or priestess anywhere. If you desire to dedicate your life to God, you become a priest or priestess. No big deal!

Why do people want to be recognized now? It is actually due to insecurities left-over from other times. If your world once harbored grudges against people of different faiths, today's world would be a totally different one. If the world of today tolerates all, it is because that work is done. You can do your thing now and few, if any, will object to it. If you do not do your work, will you settle into a rut? Obviously, you will.

We want you to understand why you threw out *The Church* before entering into another compact with it. You must finish a job before you can begin a new one. You had to earn your way in the old structure—and you did. Now you are aware that earning your way is not what was intended, rather a misinterpretation of the counsel given by God.

You must earn your life, but not physically. You can earn your way by never earning a penny. Earning money does not insure you earn your way to the next plane. It can even stand in your way.

What you do now is your decision, but if you wish to earn extra points, you could work on establishing a trust between you and the work of others, so you can work together. If you can work together, you have a church. It need not be a building or co-operative venture. It need not be in the world of work or even here on Earth, but you have to form cooperative alliances before you can begin to advance to the next plane. It is the way of the universe.

What you do now is totally your decision. You decide to adopt some of the principles we condone or stop listening—and then never give it another thought. Why are you hesitating now?

It is difficult to assume responsibility for your actions and feel confident. You want to feel confident! You want to enjoy high self-esteem. You want all that you see or hear about, because basically you are greedy. If you can endure pain and suffering in order to look better, but cannot endure the pain of psychic or spiritual growth, you will be back.

If your life puzzles you, you may not know who you are when you return, but you still return. A puzzle has a solution. Once puzzles cease to interest you, you have become a solution. You can help others dissolve their fears and begin learning other things.

We cannot do much for you while here, but you can. Do it and learn! Once you learn it, it is yours forever. Each lesson adopted by *you* is there forever—be sure you know it!

We will let you memorize your lessons now or write out your thoughts in a journal. Do whatever you do once you start thinking, but do something NOW! If you cannot memorize, you have too much data within you already to take on more. You need to download somewhere all the old data in order to accept new. Be sure you do that soon.

Chapter Thirteen

The only time you can become all you wish to be is when you complete all you have to do. You may not know what you must do, so better begin working on you now. If you cannot figure out why you are here, meditate on it immediately!

It is the nature of man to reject the method most likely to lead to success. Figure out why people go after those who will surely demoralize or disfigure them and you have an idea of what life did to you and your mind. See if you can identify the means by which most people learn and you will find it is by way of contemplation of facts and figures, then letting it sink into the brain; but ask people how they learn and they will tell you it is by doing rather than prior study.

We question if you know yourselves at all. Why not meditate? It is the only sure method to start delving into the inner self, and it takes the least amount of time and energy.

You may energize yourself or not desire energy at all, but you get energy when you meditate by not moving about. The mind is quiet, the body is relaxed, and your spirit is allowed time to heal. Why would you deny yourself time for spiritual work? You are afraid of it!

If you fear the '*devil*' or a demon will encourage you to stray from God, nonsense! Such stories do not sound sane to a schoolboy, yet adults sit and discuss demons as though they exist. Why?

Why do you scare yourself? Because you are lazy! You do not want to work. If something takes courage or consistency of method and hard work, you want to say it is not good to do. You can scare yourself away from life, but life remains, as well as the need for meditation.

You need to mature and develop a spiritual life if you are to grow. To believe you can do otherwise is a fool's dilemma. You either believe in God and advance to higher work, or you do not believe and continue to return to Earth to repeat this work. If you never learn to feed the soul, you continue to return. You deliberately tease and condemn yourself to another and yet another life of endless repetition.

The soul of anyone is the heart of all, but not the heart. The heart is a pump designed to keep blood circulating with no apparent input into the body or the mind other than that function. If the heart stops pumping, it is okay to remove one pump and put in another with no damage done to the body, mind, or spirit; but attempt to change the brain and much damage is done to the body, mind, and spirit. We will help you understand why that is, but not now.

We are attempting to conceal nothing from you about time so you can learn to use this concept to its fullest—and begin to learn to live without it now. The time of day has little to do with *you*. You have no set time to sleep or eat, but your body prefers a regular schedule. Your mind is never hungry—except for data, and your Spirit never hungers for food, but loves companionship with others of like spirit.

If you live in a loving environment, you do not need much food. If not the case, remember food is no substitute. To live in an environment where all are at each other constantly striving to live better or in competition with one another is aggravating to the digestive system. It is hard to improve anything if your digestion is not as great as it should be. You alone end what you begin. Living in competition, you lose; but if living in harmony, you can compete.

No big deal to sit and stare at the floor and do nothing, but it is difficult to stare at the floor and clear your mind of everything. The mind tries to fill space within your spirit. You must concentrate and live in the moment, chasing away all extraneous details and worries that try to intrude.

Before you can be calm, you have to settle your body, which is not easy if you are in any way nervous, tense, or anxious. You need a calm, relaxing atmosphere of love—and then live there. Once you live in a beautiful, relaxing atmosphere of love, you cannot survive long outside of it. You *have* to return to it frequently. We want you to build such a home and live in it now.

It is simple to establish your own special haven. Select a spot where all others are discouraged from entering, then get a few supplies that give you comfort—such as a candle, incense, music, perhaps an easy chair. Sit amidst this until you feel you own it. It may take several weeks until you feel completely alone, but it will happen. You can then relax anytime you sit there—even if there is disharmony all around you.

Some work where they could easily establish such a haven. Why not do it? To the uninitiated it is not noticeable, and to those who recognize it for what it is, you are established as being wise. You have nothing to lose by trying it out for size.

Why bother with anyone who carries tales about you telling of your weaknesses or frailties? You cannot control your need to be liked by everyone. That is a need that surpasses wisdom in many instances—yet is stupid. You may even deliberately strengthen such ties in order to avoid being disliked, but it cannot help. You only decentralize your life and siphon off precious energy into channels where nothing productive will be generated.

You need to sort through all your needs and eliminate any of no use now. If your friends are not *friends*, you misplaced your trust and will live to regret it; but if friends are truly *friends*, they will not remain outside your circle even if you move.

You need to move from time-to-time to discover who sticks and who does not. If your friends lose touch from time-to-time, so what? If you lose touch, you are saying you do not care for them. Begin noticing such nuances that direct the progress of your life on Earth.

You do make progress!

You try to begin and end at the same point, but have to improve somewhere along the way to maintain your equilibrium. The backlash of life is so severe you need to do a lot to maintain the pace, but to do nothing ends with you behind where you started. It is important to sample many people before settling down on one friend, but one friend is all you need to develop.

If your relationships with others are deep, you are deep, too. If you are a shallow person, you cannot have deep relationships, even if you wish it. Your depth of spirit determines the depth of any relationship.

Before the time arrives to end your episode on Earth, you will have had many opportunities to form so many relationships that even we cannot count them all—but actually form only a few of them. Why? You seek out only those you can trust!

If your trust in self is nonexistent—which is true for more and more every day—you will not trust anyone else, either. It is true, you cannot form a relationship then! You must believe in *you* before you can believe another can love you. If you hate yourself or believe you are inferior to all others, you cannot love anyone else—including your parents, who are the closest to you of all people on Earth—whether you believe it or not.

Only you know who you are. From time-to-time you have to adopt other guises to protect your ambitions and desires—not to protect *you*. God is not about to let another being try to enter or alter *you* in any way. Only you can let others into your mind, body, or heart by letting them enter and take you away.

If you are raped or entered into violently by someone you know, do you blame yourself? Yes. You know deep within that you trusted the wrong person. You did not admit your fear and dissolve it then.

Some are harmed by violence, yet not disturbed too much by it, while others are damaged beyond repair. Why? The one who realizes the incident was a freak accident and could have happened to anyone is not so likely to blame self, while the one who is open to evil people or converses with them in a lascivious or demoralizing way is likely to take on full blame for the incident.

To never blame yourself for misbehavior, you need to conduct yourself in a blameless way all this life. *You* are the most severe critic you will ever have here. You need to believe you did not deserve the criticism if it is to not bother you. If you act and do it in, you begin to know *you* only then—but it can be a starting point.

You must put your life into perspective as soon as possible. The teen years are the best time to sort through childhood memories and leave them behind one-by-one. You can do it later if you delay, but if you do it in a timely manner, your life will be on schedule to complete each stage on time.

Adolescence is a time of growth for the body, not spirit. It takes much time to grow dense bones and strong muscles, which is the basis for health for an entire life. If hormones are strong enough, sex is a factor, but usually not. Your societies enforce a strong interest in sex at too early an age—to insure your children will marry, but it is being subverted now and unable to take place.

Couples are not permitted to marry, rather encouraged to contribute to delinquency in minors and others. Your society at heart does not like children, but unwilling to admit it. The fruit of this crop is being harvested and adults are ashamed of it—but not enough!

When you have a child it is your child for life. You may not have to support or enjoy it, but you have a child whether or not anyone else knows about it. The child has no need of two parents, but if something should happen to that parent, one parent is not as easily replaced as would be the case if there are two parents in place.

What a child needs is dependability and security. If you cannot give that to a child, the child would be better off in an orphanage. You are shocked, yet do little to change the situation. Why are there so few schools for children whose parents work? Why are children left at home alone? Why are children beaten and abused? Why are children raping and killing each other? Adults are not interested in them!

In your society you do not see animals mistreated as much as children are abused. Why? As a nation, you love animals. You trust animals as individuals. You believe they are separate beings worthy of respect, but you do not see children that way because your society is rotten!

Why would you let all you love go into the hopper to be ground into sawdust? You do not *really* love others or you. Your love of self is what determines the degree of love you can share with others. It is your choice whether or not you can be of use to society, but to abuse the young is the worst offense known to God—second only to abusing your elders.

What compensation will you give for having lived on Earth and letting others destroy it, abuse elders and children, and rape your women? We cannot see how anyone can be totally excused from these offenses now. Can you?

You need to thoroughly review *you* to see where you are negligent or disinterested. You will discover more about yourself than if you were to let these offenses go. You cannot rationalize and say to yourself, *"If I did anything now, it would only make matters worse."* If you know such things are going on, you have no excuse.

Why do people abuse children? They are inferior to children and wish to abase them. How can an adult be inferior to a child? The child is still a spiritual being, while the adult permits body and mind to take control. Spirit is an awesome thing. Your spirit is grand and glorious while the body is mundane and the mind whimsical. Children are spiritual by nature and adults admire, envy and desire that quality. Some even kill to release their anger and jealousy of the child's spirit. Of course, those who kill children, have no rescue.

When the soul of another is attacked, it is the spirit that demands recompense and will be paid. If the body is attacked, it is the mind that seeks revenge. You need never seek revenge for attacks on your soul! The God above and beyond this universe is in action and heeds any degree of abuse taking place anywhere within the universe. The swift action of this force is enough to take away the life of the culprit, but most often takes the most honored or valuable possession of that one.

You cannot seek revenge. God is the only one to mete out justice. Man is totally incapable of justice.

What you need now is a towel. You need to work up a sweat and shower or bathe after working hard. Once you are cleansed of water that collects beneath the surface of your skin, you can begin seeking the real *you*. The water is only skin deep. You do not go deep within to pump out sweat. You merely exercise the skin, so why work on it so much? Only you know, we have no idea.

What about the muscles of your mind? Do you have any? We think of your brain as a muscle, but unusual in its composition. If you exercise your mind, you will gain access to retained information much more quickly than others; but if you do not exercise your mind, it is still there. You may not have to go to the well often, but it is still there and still full.

Why not let your brain rot? It would be a waste to do so. It would result in living less than you otherwise could. It would result in being crippled. Your life would be less than it could be. Why let your spirit rot?

If you let all your life go until the end before evaluating all your dealings and people you met, you may go into a comatose state that could last for years. Instead, enter data and review it constantly, shred the old stuff and enter new experiences as often as possible to override the old and introduce new ideals. If your life is lived to the fullest possible extent, you will not linger.

Why not gain access to your inner dwelling? You are afraid. You think you could enter into spirit and never find your way back, which is the silliest of all reasons. Would you have to go deep? You are nearly as shallow as the water in a basin, and only if a basin is full can you drown in it.

You need to rid yourself of conceit

Today the world is full of self-conceit, or if you wish to be faddish, self-esteem. Everyone is in search of moral truth and righteousness from others—not from within. Why expect everyone else to be true if you are false? You think they owe it to you; you believe you are owed time and life; and if life is not well lived, it is someone else's fault.

Your life on Earth is your life! You live and breathe it—and are here to learn. No big deal! If you try to rule, you will be humbled, you cannot rule. God is the ruler of all.

Every time someone sets up to rule any domain, others rush in to destroy it. That is jealousy and rage—not wisdom—in action. God takes time to decide the best way to depose a ruler, and it takes place when it takes place.

Let God into your hearth and your home is on fire. You need to begin enjoying life and living according to God. Why God? God is!

Some Buddhists today say they do not believe in God because Buddha did not. Nonsense! Buddha preached and practiced God is. No debate, accepted as fact. Why would Buddha be honored today if God did not approve his teachings?

You now know many new things, but time continues to slip through your mind. Why? You do not like to think about conceptual matters. You like to rest, so we feel it is necessary to help you gain control of all aspects of life as you rest. It is now time to hit the concept again!

Time is not a thing. Time is! Time is the concept of God in a different form. You need time to understand God is not a thing or way of life. God is! If you grasp that, you have all you need to live.

Whatever you do now, put your work in the way of all people. You need to do *your* spiritual work. You need to do physical work. You need to study. If you let others work out on you, you lose. Honor such people by not working out on them.

Sharing insights can be of use, but often develops into a form of spiritual competition. We abhor such displays of rank. If you advance yourself, you will be put back.

Only God is—others are of God
You must recognize the difference

If your time is wasted, your life is also wasted. Begin to realize time and money are means by which you control you. If you are out of control, you are out of control. If you save money and time, you save. If you string out time in endless plans that never come to be, your life is lived the same way. If you spend money you do not have, your life is spent on things that never come to be. **Remember:** Life is like time!

If your time and life are alike, how do you recognize the passing of a day and hour in your life? You do not. You cannot remember time. How do you expect to remember it when your life changes? You must check on life from *'time-to-time'* or let it slip beyond your grasp.

How you live is your decision and choice, but how you use time determines your place in this world. It is not your choice, but it is the general consensus of all within your world to use time to modify all things, but you could all decide to change that now.

God is not changeable. God is. If you try to change God to suit your world, your world is destroyed. Time is not a destroyer of life, but God is. You need time to know you are of God, but God is. Only you need time.

Chapter Fourteen

The time to be yourself is now—not after you are through here. You need to occasionally look out at the world and see if you fit in, but seldom worry if you do not. It is the world that changes shape—not you.

You gain a certain degree of polish working in the world that comes off when no longer employed or entering it much, but it comes back easily if you pick up the pieces again. Be sure to occasionally contact the old ways, but keep your eyes on the future as you live today.

Your life is only a picture of you. It is not *you* or your work. It is the frame in which you are displayed and any work you do colors it, but in no way fills it. You will be unable to endure life if you do not always live and enjoy it. A little bit of drama goes a long way toward evening up a happy life, but life is not happy if you insist on dramatizing every step along the way. You depress only yourself—not others, since they can run from you.

Why would you sit and moan and groan? You think others will pity you, but they do not. They shun you. You become an irritating moment in an otherwise bright life. You then are not who they want to be around. You irritate others then, but you do not make anyone envious, which is what you would like to do.

Envy and jealousy come together in some people in a dangerous combination that destroys them and any happiness in their lives, but it seldom destroys those they envy. Why? Because negativity attracts negativity—and not the way to live.

If you want to be attacked, enter the arena of life. Do not sit at home with loved ones. If loved ones attack, you have no place to go but within to find peace; therefore, those attacked in this life are in the best position to learn of God and develop themselves as far as they can. So do not fear attacks, they develop you far more than love does.

Love is the source of inspiration, but it builds none of the characteristics of endurance. If you are to have strength and durability for a long life of success, you must be challenged to build along lines you show as weakness. Love is hope, and fear is of the past—put them together to have a well-balanced personality.

When you see how little time you have on Earth compared to *all time*, you recognize this is not the end of one life and the beginning of another, rather an episode or one segment that leads to another and another until the soul is one with God. You do not need to be anyone else to learn every lesson. You need not live several lives to learn all the lessons, either. It takes only one very full, well-rounded life to live all the lessons of life. Be sure you experience as much as possible in order to advance to the next plane this time.

This time is a phrase often employed by the weak. It is an ultimatum of sorts. "*You can do it this time, but...*" is a weak, ineffectual comment on the speaker's state of mind and lets others off the hook. It accomplishes nothing. To be true to *you*, make your demands stick or do not make them!

In the work world there are those who never question a superior, because it might make them look stupid. Why would you not ask your superiors? Your peers or those below you know less than you do. Do not ask for information from people who know less than you, it will misinform you.

You are the source of worldly information for your Spiritual Guides—who listen to you. Why ask for old data when new exists? Why ask people who know as much or less than you? Laziness enters work when you are sure you do not know and cannot find out. You must leave it behind, or it will ruin your life.

If your life is not well thought of by you, how do you think others see it? We believe others are far more critical or far less, but seldom accurate in their appraisal of you. Do not expect feedback to be exactly true. You need it, but you need to evaluate your own work more.

There are many hours and days in the time of your life that blend into one another. Why? Because you do not finish work. You need to entirely finish work before you can move to the next stage.

If you enter school as a child and complete it as an old man, what did you learn? You learned nothing about the world or lives of average people. You learned only facts written by others living in the world who expect you to have some experience in it. It is not wise to study all your life and never live it. Life ends too soon.

If your time is limited, you know you must get your priorities in line—and you do. We are unable to understand what you need to get ahead, but we can help you once you know. If all your priorities are in line, we check them off one-by-one. If you are lost, we let you alone until you get back on track.

We do not direct you, nor do your Guides. If you are not in touch with us, you are lost for as long as it takes you to acknowledge wisdom and seek help. Why would we, or your Guides, never lead you? We are not here to help you. We are here to assist you in any way we can. You, however, are here to do your work.

If you do not know where to go—ask. If your life is in danger, call upon the angels; however, so many call upon angels today that you might believe the whole world is in danger. Stop calling upon angels if your life is not in danger!

You are to call upon God for help, and the first line of such help is your Spiritual Guides, then others of whatever category you request assistance. We are teachers and help those who ask questions or seek knowledge. We do not give vital understanding of the intricacies of your personal spiritual life. Your Guides are there to help you connect to what you need.

When the time comes for you to end your life on Earth, you will. To end your life by committing suicide is not the way to leave! If you do, you will be forced to return—or maybe lose your soul. Weakness and stupidity often cause people to fear life, but life is nothing to fear. It is *you*. You are life and change every day in every way.

Work is what you do. You need to work. Your work never ends, but each day you finish having done something. That is how you live your life. Each day leads you further toward the end. You do not work hard if you know your work is for someone else. Remember, it is your work, so do it NOW! If you suggest you are not hurting anyone by not working, you slack off. You then hurt you.

When your life is complete and you no longer wish to stay here, ask for help. Everyone does. If you suspect you will be different, you are the supreme egoist you have always been and unable to leave easily. Egoists have the hardest time dying. Why? They do not believe anyone is more powerful than themselves. What rubbish!

If your life is finished and you are unhappy, why would you end it? You would have to reenter and do it all over again. Many here now ended their lives in other times and are back to review why they could not handle it then, which is why you seek answers now. What you knew then is still within you, but you need to ask questions to discover how much you do not know now. If you do not ask questions, you can be sure you never ended your life. You lived life fully and enjoyed what happened, thus you believe the same will be true this time, too.

Faith is the outcome of experience. If you love someone and in return are not loved, you believe everyone hates you. If you always live with another, you believe you will always live with someone. You may not want anyone else, but cannot imagine living differently. The cycle is broken only when you step outside your experience to willingly live as you do now.

You may marry or not, but you should not marry out of fear. If you live alone, you must enter many relationships to make up for the solitary one that does not explore every facet of *you*. If you are married, but refuse to converge into one relationship, and instead seek many others for stimulation, you failed in the primary relationship and continue a cycle. You need to end one cycle to begin another, but think before you do it.

All you need is time!

You never have enough time. You cannot do whatever it is because you do not have time is merely an excuse. You have time to do all you want to do! All know it—and so do you, but you keep telling yourself such nonsense hoping to convince others you are important—which does not work.

People are impressed by those who appear to have time for everyone and everything. If you cannot count, you never know how much money or time you have, so you run short. If you can count, how can you run out of money or time? Poor planning is not due to oversight, but greed. You want it all and cannot give up anything.

Greed is an ingredient in time consumption. You need a lot of time to do certain work and little for other chores. Which do you do first? Work out the details and let us help you NOW. Put your plans on paper and erase what is superfluous later. If you run out of time, the last items are left undone, so make sure the most important details are first in line.

You may want to enter life as a winner, but it takes time to be one. You must learn skills required to be one, but some take off immediately to seek fame without any skills. Why? They believe all others are fools. This is ego talking.

The artist without a school may not need one, but must practice many years to perfect the skills present. To believe otherwise is being greedy. To try to sell the fruits of one's hands to all ready to purchase, before one has developed skill, is to end up poor. You need to start small and grow. Develop a special knack or ability no one else has and produce it in ever larger numbers. To jump ahead several steps is to lose it all in the end. Life is the same.

If you lost due to poor planning, do you remember to plan the next time? You do if you are wise. If you keep making the same mistakes, you are indeed a fool. You do not need anyone to tell you.

You need to sit down and examine yourself. Can you see why you are failing or winning now? If you cannot, why would another make you see it? Blindness prevents you from being *you*.

Blind people are not necessarily without sight, but sightless people often are far more insightful than everyone around them. Why? You need to develop yourself, and if you cannot see, you work at it. To open your eyes and see is the best possible way to move quickly; but if you do not move quickly, why see?

The only order to follow is one you issue. If you do not believe in what you say, no one else will either. It may take a while, but all will leave you. You must believe it as you speak or your work is tainted. You never see or say anything others will remember if you cannot remember them. This is why large crowds are only moved by single men or women. The crowd cannot remember large numbers of people—only themselves.

When you seek help, seek it from one person at a time. Organizing a club to seek help is unwise since you will have trouble remembering who is who and who does what. If you deal with one teacher at a time, you can remember all is your work. If you go to a number of conflicting teachers, you become confused and will not remember who you are. That is why we are not a group (but actually we are). We present this material as a single entity would. You cannot remember one thing from many, but can remember many things given by one entity.

God is. God is singular. God is not a number of entities tied together to act as one. God is one. You are of God, but not a single, solitary being. You are made up of several places where you go and stay and remain, then return to this place—usually as you sleep. If you wish to know who you are, you find out bits and pieces by dream analysis, but will never know the facts until you cross over to the other side.

Why are you puzzled?

Are you here to develop into a multi-dimensional being? You already are one, and you are here to become all one particular personality can be. That is why you came to Earth; why you must work; and why you all developed time—to count how long you have until you must leave.

If your life is now over—and you think it is, you probably have a few more years left here on Earth. Seldom are you aware of the final destination or date of departure. Why? You all are afraid of death. If you knew your date of death, you would not progress. Paralyzed with fear, you would do little here.

Some see themselves as dead and act with dispatch to free themselves of death, doing many things they would not have done otherwise, but you cannot free yourself of death. You merely recognize it as it is. You do not have to fear it or be in awe of it.

Death is! You are! God is! The work of this world is not all there is. The work of God is. Why not work for God and keep your work? Your work on Earth disappears when you do—only God's work remains here.

Whatever you do, do your work first. If you have time to do something easy, do it—otherwise do the hard stuff first when young and physically strong. You never know when you might be unable to work and would then be returned to do it later.

This world's work is not permanent. It is like a blackboard: You fill it with work and then erase it, fill it again, and erase it again. So you can work, you never know when the last lesson is done. Today's world is not interested in working hard, instead it is interested in doing less and playing more. You can fall into this trap or not. It is your choice. You can fall into many traps. They are put there by you, so why fall into a trap of your making?

This is the end of the session, because we ran out of time. No, we did not. We like to say it, because you say it so often. You never run out of time, but may believe you do. Why? What is there about time that confuses you? Why would you want more time if it hurts you? Why do you use time-out to punish others in prison? You know time is needed to do all your work here. It is imprinted in your mind—not in your soul.

Get your mind in gear and have it ready to go all year. Forget yourself and you can lose track of time. It works to keep you on track, but should not hinder you from doing all you came here to do. Be on time—or not. It is your life!

Chapter Fifteen

The only time to work alone is when there are no others. You have to learn to live with others, so you might as well learn to work with them, too. Do both and enjoy the benefits of gifts and rewards that come from doing work others enjoy, too.

Enjoyment is the key to life. If you do not enjoy your life, who will? If others are unhappy, they can impact your life as well and hurt your chances of success, thus you should want others to be happy, too. How can you be happy while others suffer? You cannot, so assist them in their trials and tribulations until they are happy, too.

When you feel happy, but suspect others are not, do you ask them if they are upset? If you avoid all such confrontations, you are immature and lacking in social graces. If you ask and they say nothing, you have done all you can—let the matter rest.

The only people happy now, regardless of what happens, are those who do not fear death. All others relate back to a deep-seated fear of death. Everything they fear now relates to death. Yes, it does!

If you fear death, you do much to avoid the subject, or any appearance of fear, but it is still there. Perhaps to aggravate yourself, you become phobic, dreading things you believe could advance your death. You think others are fearsome beings, or you cannot look at them, but it all relates to being afraid of death.

If your death here is not a time of death, why do you call it that? You do not believe in eternal life! You may belong to religions or worship in traditional ways that emphasize life everlasting, but do not believe it. You think you will die when you breathe your last breath on Earth. We are here to help you learn why that is not when you die, merely a change to another phase of existence.

In the work of this world are many who are not nice to know. Why? You need to learn tolerance. If you work hard and others are not nice, you believe it is your right to do the same in return. It is not. They may not know any better, but you do.

You must tolerate the ignorant, vile, and unseemly. If you cannot tolerate all others, you have to return to Earth and become such a person. Why risk it?

Enjoy life and ignore those who are ignorant, vile, or nasty. To ignore is to tolerate but not care for the behavior of such people. It is acceptable to do that. You need to learn to ignore such people so they will change. If you acknowledge them in any way, you give them reason to continue their bad behavior.

The time to be you is when: you are the only one unhappy; you are unwilling to be happy; your life is such a mess no one can straighten it out; or you have everything in order and are happy all the time. If you fail to be *you*, your happiness cannot last. It will not endure if too shallow, so be you—it pays!

If your work of the world is ugly or shallow, you grow to look like it. Be sure to be in tune with your work. Selling your time is one thing, but selling you is totally unacceptable. The world tramples all who do that. People often sell themselves to gain recognition and fame, and no one remembers them later. Your talent or gifts can gain fame and recognition, but not self-promotion.

Extend your hands and look at them...

Do you see you in your hands? Are they pampered or abused? Can you see strength or weakness? Do you see distended veins or is your skin soft and puffy? Above all else, you need strong hands if you work. Your mind can be soft if your hands are hard-working and still make a living. If your hands cannot connect mind with eye, your life is endangered. You cannot make much of a living and are prey to others.

Pull in your hands now and put them on your lap. Do you feel pounding or throbbing? If so, you have much tension or high blood pressure. Make sure your blood pressure is relieved and lowered. You cannot work hard if your blood remains elevated in pressure or infection entered your blood stream. Be sure your blood is good.

Once your blood is cared for, the body usually can restore itself—provided there is enough oxygen and water. You need oxygen to restore your body's cells, and water to carry off waste. The only water inside your body is in your bladder, kidneys, and tissue. If you escalate drinking water, your body believes it is being flooded and will evacuate all the water it can. This is why you drink much water to lose water weight. Water can increase your blood pressure, thus needs to be released.

Do not help others until you know you are in great shape. If your body is out of shape and you feel sad, you are. You need to be in the prime of life at whatever age you are then. No time is better than another—except the present.

If you dwell in the past, your emotional stability sways toward depression. If you dwell in the future, you most likely are prone to be anxious. It is best to remain rooted in the present, venturing further into the future than the past, since you are headed in that direction, but do not become preoccupied with either the past or future. It is dangerous to lose sight of NOW!

Why not live in the past? You do not live there. You live now! How can you dwell on subjects of past interest and not lose time today? You cannot. You must live now and plan for the future. If you do not, your present is not working out the future. Because of their past, many people have no future.

Before you begin a new life, you need to sign a statement of sorts identifying why you wish to come to Earth and what you hope to accomplish, but you do not have to say when it will be done. You can state how long you believe it will take, but cannot demand life end at that time. God alone makes that decision.

How can God decide the time each person remains on Earth? You are of God and have cells in your body that indicate your expected life span here on Earth. If you heed them, you live quite long; but if you decide to indulge in habits that end life sooner, you are most likely to have bad health for quite a long time. If your life is genetically determined to be short, you can indulge and end life before it takes its toll. You never know, do you?

The work of this world is not the work of planet Earth. This planet is a living organism that lives and works in the universe the same as you; however, it is much larger and denser. You think it immaterial if the Earth lives, but you are material and made up of the same elements. Why is that true? Because you are of Earth as long as you live here. If you are of Earth and know you are of God, what does that make Earth? Think about it!

Now that waves of consciousness are receding, we can absorb how little you think. You do not consciously care about Earth, but it is you. Why would we care if you harmed Earth? Because *you* are on Earth; and if you destroy it, you will be gone before the end of this life and we will have worked with you in vain now.

The end of the world is not the end of Earth. We repeat that over and over again, but some still cannot see the difference. You are too old or upset if you cannot see the difference. Why not sit down and dream of life in the bigger scheme of things? You cannot, because you have no time? Nonsense, do it NOW!

The reason you are here is the puzzle all must solve. Some go to books to figure it out, while others do not. You can go to books for information, but you need to know what to look up. Where do you begin? How much do you need to know? How to apply it? These are questions only a student of Earth can answer.

Whatever you do on Earth is your work. Your world is created by you and others around you. It is not the same elsewhere on Earth, nor is it going to change. You can try to unite all of Earth in a common cause, but it will not prevail.

What you need more than anything is the share of knowledge you had when you arrived on Earth. You do not need hypnosis or any other kind of therapy to see why you came to Earth, but it helps. If you cannot determine the time and date of your birth, you have problems. You will learn much from the astrological charts. Today's man scoffs at this, but today's man is unhappy.

Why reject the wisdom of olden times? Ego! You believe you know it all now. You believe man has progressed far beyond times gone by, but you are wrong. Earth has known many cultures that are far superior to yours. Notice, we said, "*are*". They exist, but in a different time frame from yours now.

Now that your attention is centered, why not live like this? You can! You can keep your attention centered without being distracted by everything or every person who crosses your path. It is a matter of self-discipline. Act like an adult and you become one. Act like a child and lose status. Why? You cannot go back. You must go forward.

The time to move is when you feel you are no longer doing as much as you should do. If you cannot work, you cannot exist. If you do not exist, why remain on Earth?

You fear moving forward!

Moving is generally accepted as meaning you are changing for the better. Why? Because it is implied you are moving forward. This is the proper way to think. You need to move or you die. If your body never moves, it dies. If your brain ceases to move, you are declared dead, but may be alive. Your spirit is always moving. Get all three together and you move ahead!

In the work of the world you can develop into a big shot or nobody. It is up to your ego. If your ego demands recognition and is upset by not getting enough attention at home, you will carry it forward and try desperately to be accomplished enough to be recognized in the world. If recognition is not received, or you feel it is not enough, you become bitter. It is your ego's response to life, but it is not you.

If you let your ego determine who you are, you will have to return. You cannot let your ego or body determine why you are here or when you will leave. Suicide is a decision of the ego—not Spirit. If The Holy Spirit is set free and able to add its full dimension to your life, you will never come even close to contemplating suicide, let alone pursuing it.

To treat suicide as an emotional problem is not enough. It is a spiritual crisis demanding the attention of all members of that person's clan. If it is ignored or silenced, the individual will try again and again in order to attract attention. Try to give that soul what it needs, but not too much. If too much attention is given to anyone, it causes that soul to demand, demand, demand and that is aggravating to all of us—not just *you*.

When you see '*brats*' or spoiled adults, do you wish to slap them? It is not the physical beating of another that subdues them. It is the attempt to end their tyranny. They do not want to be out of the middle or without attention. Let them go! Ignore whenever they are self-absorbed, instead train them to be social beings or be ostracized in later life. If you doubt that, look at alienated families today.

Why do you want to be the center of your family? You want to be in charge! You want to take command. You do not want anyone else to be more popular, or you want to see what it is like to have power. All of these reasons are evil in and of themselves, but quite human. You need to examine why you would enter into the center of any circle. If you decide you are not of that circle, you need to move. If you decide you are not wanted, you need to join the circle before you move. It is a lesson in human understanding to be accepted by your peers.

Why do you sit at the side and never enter the circle? You are afraid. You fear awesome responsibility will be given that will force you to work—and you do not like work. That is when you must work. It is a lesson you must learn.

What you do and why you do it is not important unless you learn from it. What you do is for you, and why you do it is connected to the universe. The work you choose is for *you*, and why you do it is not necessarily the same. If it is, you are a winner and easily satisfied.

The losers of life are never satisfied. If you find you are constantly disappointed or dissatisfied, you need to sit and enjoy yourself. Sit and think of all the times you laughed or had success. Why? Then you know why you are unhappy now.

If you had a lot of pain and suffering at birth or shortly thereafter, you know already that this life is not one of ease; but if your life was relatively stable and unexceptional in the early years, you may believe you are not going to have any problems. This definitely sets you up for disappointment.

You are here to iron out difficulties stemming from past lives on Earth or to learn how to manipulate this environment successfully—or you are here to be *you*. All are part of the same class, but some are here for only one lesson, others for all of them. If you have only one thing to do, your life is easy compared to those who have much to do, but you can have as difficult a life as they do if you choose to make it difficult. The choice is yours!

Why would you choose to make life difficult? Your ego is in charge—ask it. Ask why you are so sure you have it harder than everyone else. Ask why you think you deserve more than others. Ask why you have never had fun or been popular, and ask why you think you should be excused from doing life's dirty work. All are ego-driven topics you need to know the answers to now if you are to move forward.

Do you believe that when your life is over, you will gain the top of the heap? If so, you should be ashamed of it. You do not have a heap to top. You have only *you*. Your life is *you*. You cannot let others enter into damaging you. It is your life and you can let anyone into it you choose, but you will not be entered by anyone without asking them to do so.

The fact that you open yourself to others is why you become distressed and upset if and when they take advantage of you. Why not close yourself off from others? You do. You keep yourself locked up tight. You fear if you open up and are not wary the world will take charge of your life. Rest assured that no one wants your life—even if you are rich and famous. No one will trade for what they have.

The only way to be open and not taken advantage of is to be you. If you are closed, you cannot learn or develop. You stay closed to the great as well as the small, and the great come in far larger numbers than the small.

If you exclude others based on religion, race, or sex, you will be unable to round out your experience while here on Earth—and will have to return. We suggest you enter your heart and sort out the real reason you fear those different from you. We know you will learn more about *you* than you know now—and you will grow.

If the work of this world is too much for you, you can ask for help. You can even ask to be released of the burden. It is up to you to ask. If you never ask, you will not receive exactly what you want.

The ego is strictly an earthly vehicle and not part of the spirit of you—but it is a totally dedicated vehicle. It will not drive you anywhere else but through the land of Earth. It is there to steer you, but you apply the brakes and accelerate. Why do you let it steer you? Because you are afraid to live. If you learn to live in Spirit, you do not need much ego to survive.

The time has come to enter the next work, and you have not learned this one! How can you find time to go forward if you cannot find time to do this work? It is your problem. You must solve it before you can leave Earth. We will help if you ask, but it is your life!

In the next work we will not be as concerned about your problems. We will concentrate on how to manipulate the world in order to survive and succeed, but you need to know why time is and how to use time, before you can proceed to that work. Be ready!

Ruth Lee, Scribe
Dictated by *The Teachers of the Higher Planes*
Spring, 1994
Revised for Today's Readers, Fall 2016

Have You Read

We Are Here

The First Book of Wisdom

There is more to living and dying than human beings realize while here on Earth. Are you aware intelligent beings exist beyond our time and space who work diligently to teach universal truths? There are—and they are here now!

We Are Here is the work of teachers charged with educating humanity about the basic facts of life, spirituality, and ascension. Using spiritual scribe, Ruth Lee, *The Teachers of the Higher Planes* channeled material essential to living a full and meaningful life. This work is revolutionary in its straight-forward presentation of what the world needs and how each of us can achieve higher levels of love, success, and peace in every aspect of daily living right now.

The Teachers lay bare the aspects of human society which endanger all who live on Earth—even Earth itself! They provide clear instructions on how to correct the problems of our times. Shockingly frank—not at all concerned with the reaction of first-time readers.

Now is The Time, fourth in the Books of Wisdom series, provides knowledge you need to know to figure out why you are here—now at this time—and what you can do to improve your life in all ways, every day, starting NOW!

To learn more about **We Are Here ~ *The Teachers of the Higher Planes*,** as well as **Now is The Time** visit:

www.LeeWayPublishing.com

www.ingramcontent.com/pod-product-compliance
Lightning Source LLC
LaVergne TN
LVHW010918110826
845149LV00013B/2417